HENRY V

HENRY V

William Shakespeare

Edited by
CEDRIC WATTS

WORDSWORTH CLASSICS

For my husband
ANTHONY JOHN RANSON
with love from your wife, the publisher.
Eternally grateful for your unconditional love.

Readers who are interested in other titles from
Wordsworth Editions are invited to visit our website at
www.wordsworth-editions.com

For our latest list and a full mail-order service, contact
Bibliophile Books, 5 Thomas Road, London E14 7BN
TEL: +44 (0)20 7515 9222 FAX: +44 (0)20 7538 4115
E-MAIL: orders@bibliophilebooks.com
WEBSITE: www.bibliophilebooks.com

First published in 2000 by Wordsworth Editions Limited
8B East Street, Ware, Hertfordshire SG12 9HJ

ISBN 978 1 84022 421 4

Text © Wordsworth Editions Limited 2000
Introduction and Notes © Cedric Watts 2000

Wordsworth® is a registered trademark of
Wordsworth Editions Limited

Wordsworth Editions
is the company founded in 1987 by
MICHAEL TRAYLER

Typeset in Great Britain by Antony Gray
Printed and bound by Clays Ltd, St Ives plc

CONTENTS

GENERAL INTRODUCTION

The Wordsworth Classics' Shakespeare Series, with *Henry V* as its inaugural volume, presents a newly-edited sequence of William Shakespeare's works. Wordsworth Classics are inexpensive paperbacks for students and for the general reader. Each play in the Shakespeare Series is accompanied by a standard apparatus, including an introduction, explanatory notes and a glossary. The textual editing takes account of recent scholarship while giving the material a careful reappraisal. The apparatus is, however, concise rather than elaborate. We hope that the resultant volumes prove to be handy, reliable and helpful. Above all, we hope that, from Shakespeare's works, readers will derive pleasure, wisdom, provocation, challenges, and insights: insights into his culture and ours, and into the era of civilisation to which his writings have made – and continue to make – such potently influential contributions. Shakespeare's eloquence will, undoubtedly, re-echo 'in states unborn and accents yet unknown'.

CEDRIC WATTS
Series Editor

I

Shakespeare's *Henry V* has the reputation of being a great patriotic drama which celebrates one of the most charismatic monarchs in British history. To Shakespeare's contemporaries, Henry V was already this 'star of England', as the chronicles made clear.

Raphael Holinshed's *Chronicles of England, Scotland, and Ireland*, the main source of the play, says:

> This Henrie was a king, of life without spot, a prince whome all men loved, and of none disdained, a capteine against whome fortune never frowned, nor mischance once spurned . . . He had such knowledge in ordering and guiding an armie, with such a gift to encourage his people, that the Frenchmen had constant opinion he could never be vanquished in battelll . . . [F]or conclusion, a majestie was he that both lived & died a paterne in princehood, a lode-starre in honour, and mirrour of magnificence: the more highlie exalted in his life, the more deepelie lamented at his death, and famous to the world alwaie.[1]

I was first introduced to Shakespeare's *Henry V* by the Laurence Olivier film, which I saw in 1945.[2] It seemed well worth queuing for. There was the engagingly airborne opening, in which the camera curved above a model of Elizabethan London, seeking the Globe Theatre; there followed the descent into the crowded playhouse itself, and, after the splendidly declamatory opening ('O, for a Muse of fire!') there ensued a stage-play which gradually transformed itself into a panoramic war-film. How rousing, then, seemed Henry's rhetoric ('Once more unto the breach, dear

friends, once more'), how ominous the contrast between the
weary British army and the proudly resplendent French, and how
stirring the battle-scene at Agincourt, the arrows whooshing into
the sky as the French cavalry thundered into action, while William
Walton's music amplified the excitement. The cinema audience
cheered the victory and applauded at the end (before standing to
attention for the National Anthem). Well, that was Spring 1945, so
you can understand the enthusiasm. The Allies were about to
vanquish the Nazis. After the retreat from Dunkirk in 1940, after
the havoc of the Blitz, after a time when Britain had stood alone
and was in danger of invasion from Hitler's armies, the enemy was
in retreat; and now the nation could rejoice in the prospect of
victory and the resumption of peace. The Olivier film of *Henry V*
matched the mood. It reminded us that in the past, too, the
underdogs could at last prevail, and that on the continent then and
now, British troops, however diverse their origins, could unite to
defeat a formidable foe. The very richness of the film, its colour,
eloquence and spectacle, after years of austerely low-budget and
predominantly black-and-white productions for the cinema, made
you feel proud to be British.

Yes, times change. What once seemed a justifiable pride in the
nation's achievements and in brilliant leadership (whether of Henry
V, Winston Churchill, or even of Olivier as actor-director) could
from a later viewpoint look a little naïve and even suspect. When
Richard Branagh released *his* film of *Henry V* in 1989,[3] there were
marked differences in tone and implication. Branagh's Henry was
less stirringly noble: now there was a touch of harshness and even of
dementia in the characterisation; and, at the Battle of Agincourt,
the warriors screamed and hacked and clawed at each other in rain
and mud; slow-motion shots and sad music commented critically
on the mayhem. When that film was made, the Vietnam War was
still recent history, and the Falklands War (1982) was fresh in
memory. World War II, now that its full horrors were known (the
horrors not only of the Holocaust but also, for example, of the
destruction of Dresden, Hiroshima and Nagasaki), seemed not
entirely a saga of the defeat of evil Goliaths by noble Davids.
Scepticism thus infiltrated the depiction of war and of war-leaders.
But Shakespeare, who naturally took liberties with his sources,
would probably have been unsurprised by the differences. Neither

film gave the whole text; both made cuts to suit the directors' purposes; and Shakespeare's play contains, alongside its eloquent patriotism and its celebration of martial courage, a 'sub-text' of irony, scepticism and sombre realism.

Furthermore, the contrasts between the earliest texts of *Henry V* suggest the variability with which the material was deployed in the theatre in Shakespeare's own day. Increasingly it is being recognised that Shakespeare's writings for the theatre were, in his lifetime, protean scripts for the use of players; they were scripts that might be performed in one way at one location, in another way at another location; they could be adapted, cut, expanded, lent topicality, as occasion demanded. Indeed, the surviving texts resemble partly-unreliable transcripts of a work in progress, for what has been captured in print seems to be a somewhat garbled selection from a range of possible versions. Shakespeare wrote more than will ever be retrieved; and the contributions made to his plays by the actors, prompters, musicians, and, of course, the responsive audiences of that time, remain largely matters of guesswork.

2

Criticism entails scholarship, and scholarship entails criticism. To understand the play, we need to understand some features of its textual history. What at first seems to be a matter of dry scholarship proves to be laden with critical implications, with puzzles and oddities. The range of options, for actors, directors, students and critics, is wider than you might at first imagine.

The earliest printed text of the play is the First Quarto (Q1), a paperback which appeared in 1600.[4] There followed the Second and Third Quartos (Q2 and Q3, 1602 and 1619 respectively). Then, in 1623, the play appeared as part of the handsome First Folio (F1), the first collected edition of Shakespeare's plays, published seven years after the author's death; a compilation by two of his former fellow-actors, John Heminge and Henry Condell. Most modern editions of the play derive predominantly from F1, though the editors usually take some material from Q1 and occasional details from Q2 and Q3. No manuscript material has survived.

Q1 offers a short and, at times, garbled version of *Henry V*. It is often called a 'bad' quarto, meaning 'based on report and not

directly on a Shakespearian script'. What probably happened is that
two members of the acting company dictated from memory a draft
of the play, and this was then set in type.[5] The two actors are
thought to be those who played the parts of Exeter and Gower,
because those characters' speeches seem more reliable than others'.
The brevity of Q1 results partly from lapses of memory; and what
was being remembered may have been a play abbreviated perhaps
by censorship and perhaps by a need to reduce the number of actors
required (e.g. for a provincial tour). Although Q1 often appears to
give garbled versions of speeches, sometimes it provides superior
versions of passages or of details in F1. Q2 and Q3 are reprints of Q1
with a sprinkling of small corrections and alterations.

F1 is thought to have been set in type from Shakespeare's 'foul
papers' (i.e. an untidy manuscript). A playhouse transcript may also
have contributed, and the printers of F1 may have consulted Q3.
Generally F1 offers speeches which tend to be fuller and of higher
literary quality than their counterparts (where they exist) in the
earlier texts. Nevertheless, it displays evidence of changes in the
play which have not been fully co-ordinated. For instance, at the
end of Act 5, scene 1, Pistol declares that he is old and weary and
that his 'Doll' has died in hospital. Previously, there has been no
indication of age and weariness on his part: on the contrary, he has
been a vigorous spitfire of a rogue. Furthermore, he is married not
to 'Doll' but to Nell. Doll (Doll Tearsheet) was Falstaff's whore in
2 Henry IV, the previous work in the sequence of history-plays.
Some editors speculate that originally Falstaff was to have featured
as a character in Henry V; changes were made, so that his death was
(touchingly) reported and some of his speeches were given to
Pistol; but the adaptation was not completed: anomalies remain.
Again, the Chorus's Prologue which opens Act 2 says that the next
scene will be set in Southampton; a few lines later, in a couplet that
looks like an afterthought, it says that the location shifts to
Southampton – but only when the King comes forth; and the
following scene is actually located in London. Another instance: at
the end of Act 3, scene 5, the French King insists that the 'Dolphin'
(Dauphin) must not go to Agincourt but must remain at Roan
(Rouen); nevertheless, two scenes later, the Dolphin turns up at
Agincourt, boasting of the horse which has inspired him to write a
sonnet. In the counterpart-scene in Q1, his place is taken by

'Burbon' (Bourbon), who similarly is inspired by a beloved horse. If you read the play in the Arden text edited by T. W. Craik, you find that scene 7 of Act 3 includes the Dolphin, for the editor has here privileged F1. If you read it in the Oxford text edited by Gary Taylor, you find that the scene features Bourbon instead, for the editor believes that here Q1 represents Shakespeare's second (and better) thoughts.[6] Therefore, one's sense of the significance and character of the Dolphin will vary according to the editions one reads; and these vary in accordance with the significance placed by the editors on the differences between Q1 and F1. His title, too, varies, as modernisation vies with authenticity. Most editions say 'Dauphin'; the present edition, like a few others, says 'Dolphin', preserving the spelling of both those early texts.

Probably the most remarkable textual feature of the First Folio version appears in the Prologue to Act 5. We are told that the people of London welcomed King Henry on his return from France; and the speech continues:

> As, by a lower but loving likelihood,
> Were now the General of our gracious Empress –
> As in good time he may – from Ireland coming,
> Bringing rebellion broachèd on his sword,
> How many would the peaceful city quit
> To welcome him! Much more, and much more cause,
> Did they this Harry.

There's a scholarly consensus that the 'General of our gracious Empress' is Robert Devereux, the illustrious Earl of Essex.[7] On 27 March 1599, he had set out from London to suppress the Earl of Tyrone's 'rebellion' in Ireland. He failed, incurring the enmity of Queen Elizabeth, and arrived back in London on 28 September of the same year. It follows that this passage must have been written after 27 March but before the knowledge of Essex's failure reached London, around midsummer. Accordingly, scholars think that much of the play was written early in that year. One editor remarks: '[C]ompletion of Shakespeare's play can be firmly dated from January to June 1599'.[8]

The implications of the allusion to Essex are considerable. First, it proves that Shakespeare's history plays, while dealing with the past, had clear relevance to contemporaneous events. In this case, audiences were encouraged to relate Henry's successful French campaign of 1415 to Essex's rôle in the colonial struggle in Ireland. Without doubt, Shakespeare here supports that struggle to maintain English dominance abroad. Of course, there is an element of tact and prudence in the allusion. Essex's share of the comparison (though to be regarded affectionately) is 'lower' than Henry's; and the crowds had 'much more cause' to welcome the victorious Henry than they may have to welcome the returning Essex. In hindsight, the reference is highly ironic. Essex, having failed in his Irish mission, became a discredited malcontent. On 8 February 1601 he led a small band of supporters through London, hoping to stage a *coup d'état* against Elizabeth's counsellors. The attempted *coup* was another failure, and Essex was executed on February 25th. His supporters, on the eve of his uprising, had paid Shakespeare's company for a special production of *Richard II*: evidently they thought that a play about the deposition (and subsequent murder) of a monarch would help their cause. The Queen is reported to have remarked: 'I am Richard II[:] know ye not that?'[9]

Another remarkable aspect is that the topical allusion to Essex remained in the text of *Henry V* as published in 1623. You would think that it was, by then, clearly out of date, overtaken by events, and politically embarrassing to Shakespeare's company. Yet it remained. It would surely have been omitted from actual stage productions after the summer of 1599. What its survival suggests is that even the relatively good text published in the First Folio does not represent any 'final' version of the play, and that the compilers of the Folio were not particularly attentive to details of the material that they assembled. Evidently, performances not only of *Henry V* but also of other Shakespearian plays were augmented by topical details as opportunities arose or were pruned of them as circumstances changed. The F1 text offers one of numerous conceivable versions of Shakespeare's *Henry V*. Perhaps the deity presiding over Shakespeare's drama is Proteus, the god who eludes capture by constantly changing his shape.

3

It follows from what has been said in section 2 that any discussion of the nature of *Henry V* must have an element of provisionality. If we did not have the factual information that *Richard II* was regarded by some as an incentive to rebellion, we might well under-estimate the ambiguity of that play. *Henry V* has a deservedly high reputation as a patriotic drama; and its heroic rhetoric, particularly the 'Crispin Crispian' speech, can still be stirringly effective. War, though vile, is sometimes the lesser of two evils; co-ordinated courage against a formidable enemy deserves some honour; and patriotism is not always 'the last refuge of a scoundrel'.[10] The play offers an anthology of famous (and eminently quotable) patriotic, nationalistic and martial orations. As a study of the 'ideal monarch', a king who is astute, courageous, charismatic and complex, *Henry V* remains fascinating. Various features, however, can now seem embarrassing in the light of today's political sensitivities and prejudices.

In Act 3, scene 7, leaders of the French forces are depicted as arrogant and patronisingly over-confident in their view of the British. In Act 4, scene 1, in contrast, Henry, walking about the camp on the eve of battle, is seen as reflective, introspective (at times anxiously so), concerned to reason with his men on matters of moral responsibility, and piously aware that the outcome depends ultimately on the will of God. The battle, in spite of the overwhelming French superiority in numbers, results in an astonishing victory for the British.[11] It seems to be virtually miraculous. Henry emphasises repeatedly that the hand of God was here, supporting England's cause. To Elizabethans, politics and religion were symbiotic, interdependent. What was piety to them may be regarded as 'mystification', as superstitious propaganda, by a modern reader influenced by sceptical propaganda.

Such a reader, however, particularly if he or she be politically left-wing, may well be gratified by what could be construed as 'the sceptical sub-text' of the play. Consider the following materials. In Act 1, scene 2, Henry seeks assurance from the churchmen (the Archbishop of Canterbury and the Bishop of Ely) that his claim to the throne of France is valid; and they duly provide it. But Act 1, scene 1, had shown that the churchmen have an ulterior motive.

They know that the Church's wealth is threatened by a parliamen-
tary bill; and the way to avert the threat is to support Henry's claim.
Thus, from the start, we are alerted to the fact that their rationale of
the war is to be distrusted. (In any case, readers or playgoers who
know *2 Henry IV* will recall that Henry IV had advised his son to
'busy giddy minds with foreign quarrels': keep order at home by
directing attention to enemies abroad.) When the Archbishop of
Canterbury, in Act 1, scene 2, provides Henry V with the legal
justification of the French campaign, it takes the form of a tedious
rigmarole: a speech of legalistic prolixity verging on gobbledy-
gook. (In the Olivier film, the scene descended into farce as the
churchmen's heaps of documents became muddled and fell to the
floor.)[12] We soon notice a curious feature of Henry's psychology:
he seeks to make others appear to bear the responsibility for actions
of his own. In this case, he alleges that responsibility for the French
campaign rests on the churchmen's shoulders, even though the
decision to make war is his own. Next, he tells the French
Ambassadors that the Dolphin's gift of balls has provoked the
'wasteful vengeance' to be unleashed on France. At Southampton,
on the eve of departure, he sentences three conspirators to death –
but only after eliciting from them the advice that he should be stern
rather than merciful to a malefactor, so that he can then claim that
they are responsible for his own treatment of them:

> The mercy that was quick in us but late,
> By your own counsel is suppressed and killed.

(There follows a highly implausible series of speeches by the
conspirators. Scroop, Cambridge and Grey applaud the fact that,
thanks to God, they have been caught: indeed, Cambridge and
Grey positively rejoice that their wicked plot has been detected.)[13]
Later, in France, at the siege of Harflew (Harfleur), Henry tells the
French citizens that if they do not speedily surrender the town to
the British troops, they can expect the most appalling atrocities to
take place. Maidens will be raped, old and young will be massa-
cred, and even 'naked infants' will be 'spitted upon pikes'. And
who will be to blame? According to Henry, the citizens: '[Y]ou
yourselves are cause'. He's doing it again! On the night preceding
the Battle of Agincourt, Williams emphasises the heavy burden of
moral responsibility that the King bears; but, predictably, Henry is

keen to argue that if men who die in battle go to hell (because they die suddenly with their sins upon them), the blame rests not on the King who ordered them into battle but on the individuals. Eventually, when the battle is won, it is not only piety but also psychological necessity that presses Henry to give the credit for the victory (and, by implication, responsibility for the slaughter) to God Himself.

We gradually perceive that Henry, intelligent and guilt-laden, has been seeking to resolve inner tensions and deflect responsibility. One problem for him is how to reconcile the rôles of a martial king and a Christian king. Potentially there is a conflict between the two rôles, given the Christian commandment 'Thou shalt not kill', and given Christ's emphasis on turning the other cheek. Another problem for him is this. He demands loyalty and punishes rebels; yet he himself is the son of a usurper who had successfully rebelled against Richard. (That he had no legitimate right to the British throne undermines his claim to the French throne. Richard's true heir was Edmund Mortimer, Earl of March.) Henry's awareness of inner conflict emerges clearly, just before the Battle of Agincourt, in the anguished speech in which he says:

> Not today, O Lord,
> O, not today, think not upon the fault
> My father made in compassing the crown.
> I Richard's body have interrèd new,
> And on it have bestowed more contrite tears
> Than from it issued forcèd drops of blood.
> . . . More will I do;
> Though all that I can do is nothing worth,
> Since that my penitence comes after all,
> Imploring pardon.

There he recognises that if he were truly penitent, he would not be on the throne at all. He is seeking God's favour while yet clinging to ill-gotten gains, the throne and regal power.

Well, the British gain their victory, so it looks as though God has smiled on Henry after all. Henry IV was punished (by recurrent rebellions and by domestic worries) for his act of usurpation; but now, it seems, God is prepared to be reconciled to this dynasty. But the play has certainly drawn attention to contradictions in Henry

V's position and to deep divisions and tensions within the ethics of
politics and kingly rule. Part of the time, Henry seems to be a
successful unifier of realms. The point is made linguistically. In *1
Henry IV*, some important rebels against the King had non-English
accents: Glendower was picturesquely Welsh, and Douglas was a
doughty Scot. In *Henry V*, the marked accents of Fluellen, the
Welshman, Jamy, the Scot, and Macmorris, the Irishman, remind
us that Henry has united different parts of his realm against the
French. When Katherine, the French princess, receives her quaint
language-lesson, this prepares us for the eventual union: even those
French-speaking enemies will eventually (and so very gladly) be
reconciled to Henry's triumph and will accept his surging emer-
gence as King of France and Britain. Thus, a dominant part of the
play enables us to see Henry as the great unifier and eventually the
great reconciler. The marriage of Henry and Katherine will also be
the marriage of two realms, the inauguration of 'neighbourhood
and Christian-like accord':

> God, the best maker of all marriages,
> Combine your hearts in one, your realms in one.

There predominates, then, a sense of triumphant, harmonious
and divinely-blessed closure to the historical action. Nevertheless,
this play has, hitherto, repeatedly introduced discordant elements.
In Act 3, for instance, after the Chorus has referred to the British
army as 'culled and choice-drawn cavaliers', and after Henry has
said 'there is none of you so mean and base,/That hath not noble
lustre in your eyes', we are shown that the cowardly Nym and
Pistol need to be forced back into action by the angry Fluellen;
after which the Boy reflects that Bardolph, Nym and Pistol are
despicable braggarts, rogues and thieves. The Henry who sought
God's blessing on his campaign is the Henry who threatens to
unleash, on Harfleur, troops who will resemble 'Herod's bloody-
hunting slaughtermen'. 'We are no tyrant, but a Christian king',
Henry had declared, adding later: '[W]hen lenity and cruelty play
for a kingdom, the gentler gamester is the soonest winner'; but this
same advocate of lenity orders the killing of French prisoners. In
another of those textual discrepancies, this order is initially, we are
shown, a response to the news of French reinforcements. Only
tardily, and inconsistently, are we given a better rationale of this

ruthless command: namely, that French marauders have killed the baggage-boys and stolen some of the gear. Such unpredictably acerbic effects offset the predictable patriotism and piety – and even sentimentality – found elsewhere. (The deaths of the Earl of Suffolk and the Duke of York are so described as to make a sentimental cameo.) The final discord is sounded in the Epilogue. This sonnet reminds us that Henry V's achievements, though great, were short-lived. He died at an early age and was succeeded by the boy-King, Henry VI, in whose reign civil war again tore England, and France was lost. The triumphant, hopeful features of Act V are thus undercut by the poignant Epilogue, which solicits a view of history as cyclical rather than as providentially progressive, and a view of human achievements as poignantly ephemeral rather than impressively durable.

Henry V is extremely variable in quality. There are passages of rather crude and patronising comedy (notably, in the leek-eating scene), some predictable stereotyping of the French as vainglorious, some prolixity and pompous bombast, a trivialising digression into sexist humour (5.2.281–307), and a sprinkling of obscurities. On the other hand, the Chorus's frank invocations to the audience, the counterpoint of ironies, the depiction of a complex central character, the memorable rhetoric of courageous action, the lively interplay of the general and the particular, and the numerous linguistic flights into mercurial eloquence: all these guarantee the play's cultural longevity. These days, the victory of Agincourt on the day of Crispin Crispian is probably remembered less for its historical accomplishment than for its Shakespearian dramatisation. Sometimes the pen may indeed be mightier than the sword.

NOTES TO THE INTRODUCTION

1 Raphael Holinshed: *Holinshed's Chronicles of England, Scotland and Ireland* [1587] (rpt. London: Johnson *et al.*, 1807), Vol. 3, pp. 133, 134. (I have substituted the modern v and j where Holinshed used u and i.)

2 The film, commissioned by the Ministry of Information to help the war-effort, had been released in London late in 1944. It was dedicated to 'the Commandos and Airborne Troops of Great Britain'.

3 This *Henry V* was directed by Kenneth Branagh, who also played Henry; so it offered a symmetrical challenge to the Olivier version.

4 A 'quarto' is a book with relatively small pages; a 'folio' is a book with large pages. More precisely, a quarto volume is made of sheets of paper, each of which has been folded twice to form four leaves (and thus eight pages); whereas each of a folio's sheets has been folded once to yield two leaves (and thus four pages).

5 Evidence of dictation is that Q1 has numerous errors that seem to resulting from mis-hearings (e.g. 'Forage in' for 'Foraging').

6 *King Henry V*, ed. T. W. Craik (London: Routledge, 1995; rpt. Walton-on-Thames: Nelson, 1998). *Henry V*, ed. Gary Taylor (Oxford: Oxford University Press, 1982; rpt. 1998).

7 Essex was a friend of the Earl of Southampton, to whom Shakespeare had dedicated *Venus and Adonis* and *The Rape of Lucrece*. From 1601 to 1603, Southampton was imprisoned for complicity in Essex's uprising.

8 Gary Taylor, in the Introduction to his edition of *Henry V*, p. 5.

9 The Queen is quoted in *The Progresses and Public Processions of Queen Elizabeth*, ed. John Nichols, Vol. 3 (New York: Franklin, n.d.), p. 552.

10 So said Dr. Samuel Johnson in 1775. See *Boswell's Life of Johnson*, Vol. 2, ed. G. B. Hill and L. F. Powell (London: Oxford University Press, 1934), p. 348.

11 Henry is told that there are 10,000 French dead but only 29 British. Modern historians vary in their estimates, but it seems likely that deaths on the French side were about 7,000, on the British side about 500: still an astounding contrast. The battle was not, however, as decisive as the play suggests. In reality, the Treaty of Troyes (dramatised in the final scene) was not negotiated until more than four years after the slaughter at Agincourt. Meanwhile, French forces – aided by the Scots – continued to fight Henry.

12 Gary Taylor (*Henry V*, pp. 34–9) argues that the justification would, in Shakespeare's day, have been seen as both interesting and valid. Holinshed, however, in his *Chronicles*, says that the claim to France is a 'sharp invention' by the churchmen, and that the speech about the Salic Law is a 'prepared tale'. Q1 omits the scene which reveals the churchmen's self-interest: a crucial difference.

13 The play does not make explicit, as Holinshed does, that Grey was conspiring on behalf of the true heir to the throne.

FURTHER READING
(in chronological order)

E. M. W. Tillyard: *Shakespeare's History Plays*. London:
Chatto & Windus, 1944.

Derek Traversi: *Shakespeare from 'Richard II' to 'Henry V'*.
London: Hollis & Carter, 1958.

Narrative and Dramatic Sources of Shakespeare, Vol. 4, ed. Geoffrey
Bullough. London: Routledge & Kegan Paul; New York:
Columbia University Press; 1962; rpt. 1966.

F. E. Halliday: *A Shakespeare Companion*. Harmondsworth:
Penguin, 1964.

Samuel Schoenbaum: *William Shakespeare: A Compact
Documentary Life*. London and New York: Oxford
University Press, 1977; rpt. 1987.

'Introduction' to William Shakespeare's *Henry V*, ed. Gary
Taylor. Oxford: Oxford University Press, 1982; rpt. 1998.

Stephen Greenblatt: 'Invisible Bullets: Renaissance Authority and
Its Subversion, *Henry IV* and *Henry V*' in *Political Shakespeare*,
ed. Jonathan Dollimore and Alan Sinfield. Manchester:
Manchester University Press, 1985.

Jonathan Dollimore and Alan Sinfield: 'History and Ideology:
The Instance of *Henry V*' in *Alternative Shakespeares*, ed. John
Drakakis. London: Methuen, 1985.

The Cambridge Companion to Shakespeare Studies, ed. Stanley
Wells. Cambridge: Cambridge University Press, 1986.

Chapter 4 of Brian Vickers: *Appropriating Shakespeare:
Contemporary Critical Quarrels*. New Haven and London:
Yale University Press, 1993.

'Introduction' to William Shakespeare's *King Henry V*, ed. T. W. Craik. London: Routledge, 1995; rpt. Walton-on-Thames: Nelson, 1998.

Russ McDonald: *The Bedford Companion to Shakespeare*. Basingstoke: Macmillan, 1996.

A Companion to Shakespeare, ed. David Scott Kastan. Malden, Mass., and Oxford: Blackwell, 1999.

John Sutherland and Cedric Watts: *Henry V, War Criminal? And Other Shakespeare Puzzles*. Oxford: Oxford University Press, 2000.

NOTE ON SHAKESPEARE

Details of Shakespeare's early life are scanty. He was the son of a prosperous merchant of Stratford-upon-Avon, and tradition gives his date of birth as 23rd April, 1564; certainly, three days later, he was christened at the parish church. It is likely that he attended the local Grammar School but had no university education. Of his early career there is no record, though John Aubrey states that he was a country schoolmaster. In 1582 Shakespeare married Anne Hathaway, with whom he had two daughters, Susanna and Judith, and a son, Hamnet, who died in 1596. How he became involved with the stage is uncertain, but he was sufficiently established as a playwright by 1592 to be criticised in print as a challengingly versatile 'upstart Crow'. He was a leading member of the Lord Chamberlain's company, which became the King's Men on the accession of James I in 1603. Being not only a playwright and actor but also a 'sharer' (one of the owners of the company, entitled to a share of the profits), Shakespeare prospered greatly, as is proven by the numerous records of his financial transactions. Towards the end of his life he loosened his ties with London and retired to New Place, his large property in Stratford which he had bought in 1597. He died on 23rd April 1616, and is buried in the place of his baptism, Stratford's Holy Trinity Church. The earliest collected edition of his plays, the First Folio, was published in 1623, and its prefatory verse-tributes include Ben Jonson's famous declaration, 'He was not of an age, but for all time'.

ACKNOWLEDGEMENTS AND TEXTUAL NOTE

I am grateful for the expert help generously provided by Sylvère Monod of the Sorbonne and Brian Nicholas of Sussex University. Their advice on French usages has been indispensable. A useful reference-work was Randle Cotgrave's *Dictionarie of the French and English Tongues* (1611; reproduced at Menston by Scolar Press, 1968). I have consulted numerous editions of Shakespeare's play, and have given particular weight to the comments of T. W. Craik, editor of *King Henry V* in the Arden Shakespeare series (London: Routledge, 1995), and of Gary Taylor, editor of *Henry V* for Oxford World's Classics (Oxford University Press, 1998). The Glossary of the present volume builds on (but revises) that supplied by John Dover Wilson in his 1958 edition for Cambridge University Press.

When editing the play, I have taken careful account of the First Folio and First Quarto texts. Almost all modern editors of *Henry V* make a compromise between various elements, which include: (i) the material in the earliest printed versions, particularly in the highly-rated First Folio text; (ii) what Shakespeare is thought to have intended (which sometimes differs from what those texts provide); and (iii) modern conventions of spelling, punctuation and presentation. Intricate problems are offered by the passages of *Henry V* which are in French or which mention French surnames and localities. Here an editor will be aware that the early texts frequently garble Shakespeare's French; that Shakespeare's French was fallible (though sometimes he was deliberately putting errors into a character's mouth); that a modern reader may expect to read modernised French; and that the French current when the play was written often differed from the French current today. The resultant compromises by editors are usually expedient rather than elegant, with attempted fidelity to Shakespeare entailing some perfidy to the French language.

My procedures generally have been fairly conservative, in the sense that, while modernising spelling and punctuation where it seemed necessary to do so, I have given special consideration to the First Folio's authority. For instance, the First Folio text has an abundance of colons. Modern editors preserve some of these but replace many of them with a wide range of alternatives: exclamations marks, question-marks, semi-colons, commas, full stops. I have preserved a larger proportion of colons than is customary, my rule being that if the colon makes sufficient grammatical and/or rhetorical sense, it should be preserved. Similarly, I have retained various round brackets from the Folio, noting that some bracketed statements may constitute asides or *sotto voce* utterances. In the treatment of the French, I have again been relatively conservative. Consider, for example, the matter of 'Dolphin *versus* Dauphin'. The French King's heir is designated 'the Dauphin' in most modern texts, because that is the familiar modern version of the title. On the other hand, the First Quarto and the First Folio consistently give 'Dolphin', and that was the generally-accepted spelling in Shakespeare's day. (In France, early spellings included 'Dalfin' and 'Daulphin'.) Furthermore, to modernise 'Dolphin' as 'Dauphin' sometimes mars Shakespeare's euphonies. For instance, look at lines 279–84 in Act 1, scene 2, of the present edition:

> But I will rise there with so full a glory
> That I will dazzle all the eyes of France,
> Yea, strike the Dolphin blind to look on us;
> And tell the pleasant prince, this mock of his
> Hath turned his balls to gun-stones, and his soul
> Shall stand sore chargèd for the wasteful vengeance . . .

Notice how prominent in these lines are alliterative and assonantal patterns containing the sounds of 'Dolphin'. If you substitute 'Dauphin' (and imagine the modern French pronunciation that it invokes), the re-echoing 'd' and 'f' sounds are preserved, but the original 'ol' and 'i' sounds are lost, and patterns of euphony are thereby weakened. For instance, the 'ol' of 'Dolphin' resonates sounds of 'will dazzle all', 'tell the pleasant prince, this mock', 'balls', 'soul' 'wasteful'; while the 'i' of '-phin' is echoed in 'will', 'with', 'prince', 'this' and the repeated 'his'. Related considerations have resulted in my retention of the First Folio's 'Harflew', 'Callice' and 'Roan' (in place of the modern 'Harfleur', 'Calais' and 'Rouen'). The dialogues in French have been mildly modernised (so that 'anglais', for example, replaces 'Anglois'); but various grammatical errors have been preserved there, the notes providing a range of corrections.

In short, my general rule has been to preserve the First Folio material unless there are good reasons to depart from it. Chief among the good reasons for local departures has been the need to produce a text which will be adequately intelligible to the modern reader. I hope that the resultant compromise between the old texts, Shakespeare's intentions (so far as they can be reasonably inferred) and modern requirements will prove reasonable and useful. Again, the notes appended to the play draw attention to some of the more contentious or disputable passages. In any case, as you read the play, you will find that to some extent you are editing it to suit yourself, even as you are directing it in your imagination. Over to you.

HENRY V

scene: first England, then France.

CHARACTERS IN THE PLAY

KING HENRY THE FIFTH
HUMPHREY, DUKE OF GLOUCESTER
JOHN OF LANCASTER, DUKE OF BEDFORD } brothers to
THOMAS OF LANCASTER, DUKE OF CLARENCE } the King
DUKE OF EXETER, *uncle to the King*
DUKE OF YORK, *cousin to the King, formerly Aumerle*
EARLS OF SALISBURY, WESTMORLAND, *and* WARWICK
ARCHBISHOP OF CANTERBURY
BISHOP OF ELY
EARL OF CAMBRIDGE
LORD SCROOP
SIR THOMAS GREY
SIR THOMAS ERPINGHAM, GOWER, FLUELLEN,
  MACMORRIS, JAMY, *officers in King Henry's army*
BATES, COURT, WILLIAMS, *soldiers in the same*
PISTOL, NYM, BARDOLPH
BOY
Herald
CHARLES *the Sixth, King of France*
LEWIS, *the Dolphin (Dauphin)*
DUKES OF BURGUNDY, ORLEANCE, BRITAINE *and* BOURBON
The Constable of France
RAMBURES *and* GRANDPRÉ, *French Lords*
Governor of Harflew (Harfleur)
MONTJOY, *a French herald*
Ambassadors to the King of England

ISABEL, *Queen of France*
KATHERINE, *daughter to Charles and Isabel*
ALICE, *a lady attending upon her*
HOSTESS, *formerly Mrs Quickly, now Pistol's wife*

*Lords, Ladies, Officers, French and English Soldiers,
  Messengers, and Attendants*

HENRY V

ACT I. PROLOGUE.

Enter CHORUS.

CHORUS   O for a Muse of fire, that would ascend
              The brightest heaven of invention!
              A kingdom for a stage, princes to act,
              And monarchs to behold the swelling scene!
              Then should the warlike Harry, like himself,
              Assume the port of Mars, and at his heels
              (Leashed in, like hounds) should Famine, Sword,
                                            and Fire
              Crouch for employment. But pardon, gentles all,
              The flat unraisèd spirits[1] that hath dared,
              On this unworthy scaffold, to bring forth   10
              So great an object. Can this cockpit hold
              The vasty fields of France? Or may we cram
              Within this wooden O the very casques
              That did affright the air at Agincourt?
              O, pardon: since a crooked figure may
              Attest in little place a million;[2]
              And let us, ciphers to this great accompt,[3]
              On your imaginary forces work.
              Suppose within the girdle of these walls
              Are now confined two mighty monarchies,   20
              Whose high, upreared, and abutting fronts
              The perilous narrow ocean parts asunder.
              Piece out our imperfections with your thoughts:
              Into a thousand parts divide one man,
              And make imaginary puissance.
              Think, when we talk of horses, that you see them,
              Printing their proud hoofs i'th'receiving earth:
              For 'tis your thoughts that now must deck our kings,
              Carry them here and there; jumping o'er times;
              Turning th'accomplishment of many years   30
              Into an hour-glass: for the which supply,

Admit me Chorus to this History;
Who, Prologue-like, your humble patience pray,
Gently to hear, kindly to judge, our play.

                                              [*Exit.*

*Asking for forgiveness —
as the play deserves an
                              outstanding
                              performance.*

ACT I, SCENE I.

London. An antechamber in the King's palace.

Enter the ARCHBISHOP OF CANTERBURY *and the* BISHOP OF ELY.

CANT'BURY My lord, I'll tell you: that self bill is urged,
Which in th'eleventh year of the last King's reign
Was like, and had indeed against us passed,
But that the scambling and unquiet time
Did push it out of farther question.

ELY But how, my lord, shall we resist it now?

CANT'BURY It must be thought on. If it pass against us,
We lose the better half of our possession:
For all the temporal lands which men devout
By testament have given to the Church   10
Would they strip from us; being valued thus:
As much as would maintain, to the King's honour,
Full fifteen earls, and fifteen hundred knights,
Six thousand and two hundred good esquires;
And, to relief of lazars and weak age
Of indigent faint souls past corporal toil,
A hundred almshouses right well supplied;
And to the coffers of the King beside,
A thousand pounds by th'year: thus runs the bill.

ELY This would drink deep.

CANT'BURY   'Twould drink the cup and all. 20

ELY But what prevention?

CANT'BURY The King is full of grace and fair regard.

ELY And a true lover of the holy Church.

CANT'BURY The courses of his youth promised it not.
The breath no sooner left his father's body,
But that his wildness, mortified in him,
Seemed to die too: yea, at that very moment,
Consideration like an angel came,

And whipped th'offending Adam[4] out of him;
Leaving his body as a Paradise,   30
T'envelop and contain celestial spirits.
Never was such a sudden scholar made:
Never came reformation in a flood
With such a heady currance, scouring faults;
Nor never Hydra-headed wilfulness
So soon did lose his seat, and all at once,
As in this King.

ELY   We are blessèd in the change.

CANT'BURY Hear him but reason in divinity:
And, all-admiring, with an inward wish
You would desire the King were made a prelate.   40
Hear him debate of commonwealth affairs:
You would say, it hath been all in all his study.
List his discourse of war: and you shall hear
A fearful battle rendered you in music.
Turn him to any cause of policy,
The Gordian knot[5] of it he will unloose,
Familiar as his garter: that, when he speaks,
The air, a chartered libertine,[6] is still,
And the mute wonder lurketh in men's ears,
To steal his sweet and honeyed sentences: 50
So that the art and practic part of life
Must be the mistress to this theoric:
Which is a wonder how his Grace should glean it,
Since his addiction was to courses vain,
His companies unlettered, rude, and shallow,
His hours filled up with riots, banquets, sports;
And never noted in him any study,
Any retirement, any sequestration
From open haunts and popularity.

ELY   The strawberry grows underneath the nettle;   60
And wholesome berries thrive and ripen best,
Neighboured by fruit of baser quality:
And so the Prince obscured his contemplation
Under the veil of wildness, which (no doubt)
Grew like the summer grass, fastest by night,
Unseen, yet crescive in his faculty.

CANT'BURY It must be so; for miracles are ceased:[7]
           And therefore we must needs admit the means
           How things are perfected.
ELY   But my good lord:
           How now for mitigation of this bill   70
           Urged by the commons? Doth his Majesty
           Incline to it, or no?
CANT'BURY   He seems indifferent;
           Or rather swaying more upon our part
           Than cherishing th'exhibitors against us:
           For I have made an offer to his Majesty,
           Upon our spiritual convocation,
           And in regard of causes now in hand,
           Which I have opened to his Grace at large,
           As touching France, to give a greater sum
           Than ever at one time the clergy yet   80
           Did to his predecessors part withal.
ELY   How did this offer seem received, my lord?
CANT'BURY With good acceptance of his Majesty;
           Save that there was not time enough to hear,
           As I perceived his Grace would fain have done,
           The severals and unhidden passages
           Of his true titles to some certain dukedoms,
           And generally, to the crown and seat of France,
           Derived from Edward, his great-grandfather.[8]
ELY   What was th'impediment that broke this off?   90
CANT'BURY The French ambassador upon that instant
           Craved audience; and the hour, I think, is come
           To give him hearing: is it four o'clock?
ELY   It is.
CANT'BURY Then go we in, to know his embassy:
           Which I could with a ready guess declare,
           Before the Frenchman speak a word of it.
ELY   I'll wait upon you, and I long to hear it.

                                              [*Exeunt.*

SCENE 2.

The Presence-chamber in the palace.

Enter the KING, HUMPHREY [DUKE OF GLOUCESTER], BEDFORD,
CLARENCE, WARWICK, WESTMORLAND, EXETER *and attendants*.

KING   Where is my gracious Lord of Canterbury?
EXETER   Not here in presence.
KING   Send for him, good uncle.
WEST'LAND   Shall we call in th'ambassador, my liege?
KING   Not yet, my cousin: we would be resolved,
            Before we hear him, of some things of weight
            That task our thoughts, concerning us and France.

Enter the ARCHBISHOP OF CANTERBURY *and the* BISHOP OF ELY.

CANT'BURY   God and his angels guard your sacred throne,
            And make you long become it.
KING   Sure, we thank you.
            My learnèd lord, we pray you to proceed,
            And justly and religiously unfold   10
            Why the law Salic,[9] that they have in France,
            Or should, or should not, bar us in our claim.
            And God forbid, my dear and faithful lord,
            That you should fashion, wrest, or bow your reading,
            Or nicely charge your understanding soul
            With opening titles miscreate, whose right
            Suits not in native colours with the truth:
            For God doth know how many now in health
            Shall drop their blood in approbation
            Of what your reverence shall incite us to.   20
            Therefore take heed how you impawn our person,
            How you awake our sleeping sword of war;
            We charge you in the name of God, take heed:
            For never two such kingdoms did contend
            Without much fall of blood, whose guiltless drops
            Are every one a woe, a sore complaint
            'Gainst him whose wrongs gives edge unto the swords
            That makes such waste in brief mortality.
            Under this conjuration, speak, my lord:

For we will hear, note, and believe in heart,   30
That what you speak is in your conscience washed
As pure as sin with baptism.
CANT'BURY Then hear me, gracious sovereign, and you peers,
That owe yourselves, your lives, and services,
To this imperial throne. There is no bar
To make against your Highness' claim to France
But this, which they produce from Pharamond:
'In terram Salicam mulieres ne succedant' –
'No woman shall succeed in Salic land':
Which Salic land the French unjustly gloze   40
To be the realm of France, and Pharamond
The founder of this law and female bar.
Yet their own authors faithfully affirm
That the land Salic is in Germany,
Between the floods of Sala and of Elbe:
Where Charles the Great, having subdued the Saxons,
There left behind and settled certain French:
Who holding in disdain the German women
For some dishonest manners of their life,
Established then this law: to wit, no female   50
Should be inheritrix in Salic land:
Which Salic (as I said), 'twixt Elbe and Sala,
Is at this day in Germany called Meisen.
Then doth it well appear, the Salic law
Was not devisèd for the realm of France;
Nor did the French possess the Salic land
Until four hundred one and twenty years
After defunction of King Pharamond,
Idly supposed the founder of this law,
Who died within the year of our redemption   60
Four hundred twenty-six; and Charles the Great
Subdued the Saxons, and did seat the French
Beyond the river Sala, in the year
Eight hundred five. Besides, their writers say,
King Pepin, which deposèd Childeric,
Did, as heir general, being descended
Of Blithild, which was daughter to King Clothair,
Make claim and title to the crown of France.

Hugh Capet also, who usurped the crown
Of Charles the Duke of Lorraine, sole heir male   70
Of the true line and stock of Charles the Great,
To fine his title with some shows of truth,
Though in pure truth it was corrupt and naught,
Conveyed himself as th'heir to th'Lady Lingare,[10]
Daughter to Charlemaine, who was the son
To Lewis the Emperor, and Lewis the son
Of Charles the Great. Also King Lewis the tenth,
Who was sole heir to the usurper Capet,
Could not keep quiet in his conscience,
Wearing the crown of France, till satisfied   80
That fair Queen Isabel, his grandmother,
Was lineal of the Lady Ermengare,[11]
Daughter to Charles the foresaid Duke of Lorraine:
By the which marriage, the line of Charles the Great
Was reunited to the crown of France.
So that, as clear as is the summer's sun,
King Pepin's title and Hugh Capet's claim,
King Lewis his satisfaction, all appear
To hold in right and title of the female:
So do the kings of France unto this day.   90
Howbeit, they would hold up this Salic law
To bar your highness claiming from the female,
And rather choose to hide them in a net
Than amply to imbar their crooked titles,
Usurped from you and your progenitors.

KING   May I with right and conscience make this claim?
CANT'BURY The sin upon my head, dread sovereign:
For in the book of Numbers[12] is it writ,
When the man dies, let the inheritance
Descend unto the daughter. Gracious lord,   100
Stand for your own, unwind your bloody flag,
Look back into your mighty ancestors:
Go, my dread lord, to your great-grandsire's tomb,
From whom you claim; invoke his warlike spirit,
And your great-uncle's, Edward the Black Prince,
Who on the French ground played a tragedy,
Making defeat on the full power of France,

Whiles his most mighty father on a hill
Stood smiling to behold his lion's whelp
Forage in blood of French nobility.[13]   110
O noble English, that could entertain
With half their forces the full pride of France,
And let another half stand laughing by,
All out of work and cold for action!

ELY   Awake remembrance of these valiant dead,
And with your puissant arm renew their feats.
You are their heir, you sit upon their throne:
The blood and courage that renownèd them
Runs in your veins: and my thrice-puissant[14] liege
Is in the very May-morn of his youth,   120
Ripe for exploits and mighty enterprises.

EXETER Your brother kings and monarchs of the earth
Do all expect that you should rouse yourself,
As did the former lions of your blood.

WEST'LAND They know your Grace hath cause, and means, and might;
So hath your Highness: never king of England
Had nobles richer, and more loyal subjects,
Whose hearts have left their bodies here in England,
And lie pavilioned in the fields of France.

CANT'BURY O let their bodies follow, my dear liege,   130
With blood and sword and fire, to win your right:
In aid whereof, we of the spiritualty
Will raise your Highness such a mighty sum
As never did the clergy at one time
Bring in to any of your ancestors.

KING   We must not only arm t'invade the French,
But lay down our proportions to defend
Against the Scot, who will make road upon us
With all advantages.

CANT'BURY They of those marches, gracious sovereign,   140
Shall be a wall sufficient to defend
Our inland from the pilfering borderers.

KING   We do not mean the coursing snatchers only,
But fear the main intendment of the Scot,
Who hath been still a giddy neighbour to us:
For you shall read that my great-grandfather

Never went with his forces into France,
But that the Scot on his unfurnished kingdom
Came pouring like the tide into a breach,
With ample and brim fulness of his force,   150
Galling the gleanèd land with hot assays,
Girding, with grievous siege, castles and towns:
That England, being empty of defence,
Hath shook and trembled at th'ill neighbourhood.

CANT'BURY   She hath been then more feared than harmed, my liege:
For hear her but exampled by herself:
When all her chivalry hath been in France,
And she a mourning widow of her nobles,
She hath herself not only well defended,
But taken and impounded as a stray   160
The King of Scots:[15] whom she did send to France,
To fill King Edward's fame with prisoner kings,
And make her chronicle as rich with praise
As is the ooze and bottom of the sea
With sunken wrack and sumless treasuries.

ELY   But there's a saying very old and true:
    'If that you will France win,
      Then with Scotland first begin.'
For once the eagle (England) being in prey,
To her unguarded nest the weasel (Scot)   170
Comes sneaking, and so sucks her princely eggs,
Playing the mouse in absence of the cat,
To 'tame and havoc more than she can eat.

EXETER   It follows then, the cat must stay at home:
Yet that is but a crushed necessity,
Since we have locks to safeguard necessaries,
And pretty traps to catch the petty thieves.
While that the armèd hand doth fight abroad,
Th'advisèd head defends itself at home:
For government, though high, and low, and lower,   180
Put into parts, doth keep in one consent,
Congreeing in a full and natural close,
Like music.

CANT'BURY   Therefore doth heaven divide
The state of man in divers functions,

Setting endeavour in continual motion;
To which is fixèd, as an aim or butt,
Obedience: for so work the honey-bees,
Creatures that by a rule in nature teach
The act of order to a peopled kingdom.
They have a king, and officers of sorts: 190
Where some, like magistrates, correct at home;
Others, like merchants, venture trade abroad;
Others, like soldiers, armèd in their stings,
Make boot upon the summer's velvet buds:
Which pillage, they with merry march bring home
To the tent-royal of their emperor:
Who, busied in his majesty, surveys
The singing masons building roofs of gold,
The civil citizens kneading up the honey,
The poor mechanic porters crowding in   200
Their heavy burdens at his narrow gate,
The sad-eyed justice, with his surly hum,
Delivering o'er to executors pale
The lazy yawning drone. I this infer,
That many things, having full reference
To one consent, may work contrariously:
As many arrows loosèd several ways
Come to one mark;
As many several ways meet in one town;
As many fresh streams meet in one salt sea;   210
As many lines close in the dial's centre:
So may a thousand actions, once afoot,
End in one purpose, and be all well borne
Without defeat. Therefore to France, my liege.
Divide your happy England into four,
Whereof take you one quarter into France,
And you withal shall make all Gallia shake.
If we, with thrice such powers left at home,
Cannot defend our own doors from the dog,
Let us be worried, and our nation lose   220
The name of hardiness and policy.

KING   Call in the messengers sent from the Dolphin.[16]

Now are we well resolved, and by God's help
And yours, the noble sinews of our power,
France being ours, we'll bend it to our awe,
Or break it all to pieces. Or there we'll sit,
Ruling in large and ample empery
O'er France and all her (almost) kingly dukedoms,
Or lay these bones in an unworthy urn,
Tombless, with no remembrance over them.   230
Either our history shall with full mouth
Speak freely of our acts, or else our grave,
Like Turkish mute,[17] shall have a tongueless mouth,
Not worshipped with a waxen epitaph.[18]

                    Enter Ambassadors of France.

Now are we well prepared to know the pleasure
Of our fair cousin Dolphin: for we hear
Your greeting is from him, not from the King.
I AMBASS. May't please your Majesty to give us leave
Freely to render what we have in charge,
Or shall we sparingly show you far off   240
The Dolphin's meaning and our embassy?
KING   We are no tyrant, but a Christian king,
Unto whose grace our passion is as subject
As is our wretches fettered in our prisons;
Therefore with frank and with uncurbèd plainness
Tell us the Dolphin's mind.
I AMBASS.   Thus then, in few.
Your Highness, lately sending into France,
Did claim some certain dukedoms, in the right
Of your great predecessor, King Edward the Third.
In answer of which claim, the Prince our master   250
Says that you savour too much of your youth,
And bids you be advised: there's nought in France
That can be with a nimble galliard won:
You cannot revel into dukedoms there.
He therefore sends you, meeter for your spirit,
This tun of treasure; and, in lieu of this,
Desires you let the dukedoms that you claim
Hear no more of you. This the Dolphin speaks.

Tennis match is Weapons.

...asure, uncle?

...g *the barrel*]   Tennis-balls, my liege.

...are glad the Dolphin is so pleasant with us.   260
...s present and your pains we thank you for.
When we have matched our rackets to these balls,
We will in France (by God's grace) play a set
Shall strike his father's crown into the hazard.
Tell him, he hath made a match with such a wrangler
That all the courts of France will be disturbed
With chases. And we understand him well,
How he comes o'er us with our wilder days,
Not measuring what use we made of them.
We never valued this poor seat of England,   270
And therefore, living hence, did give ourself
To barbarous licence: as 'tis ever common
That men are merriest when they are from home.
But tell the Dolphin, I will keep my state,
Be like a king, and show my sail of greatness,
When I do rouse me in my throne of France.
For that I have laid by my majesty,
And plodded like a man for working-days;
But I will rise there with so full a glory
That I will dazzle all the eyes of France,   280
Yea, strike the Dolphin blind to look on us;
And tell the pleasant prince, this mock of his
Hath turned his balls to gun-stones, and his soul
Shall stand sore chargèd for the wasteful vengeance
That shall fly with them: for many a thousand widows
Shall this, his mock, mock out of their dear husbands;
Mock mothers from their sons, mock castles down;
And some are yet ungotten and unborn,
That shall have cause to curse the Dolphin's scorn.
But this lies all within the will of God,   290
To whom I do appeal, and in whose name,
Tell you the Dolphin, I am coming on,
To venge me as I may, and to put forth
My rightful hand in a well-hallowed cause.
So get you hence in peace; and tell the Dolphin,
His jest will savour but of shallow wit,

metaphorical Of the tennis rackets

kingship is shown

don't mess with him

When thousands weep more than did laugh at it.
Convey them with safe conduct. Fare you well.

            [Exeunt Ambassadors.

EXETER This was a merry message.
KING We hope to make the sender blush at it.   300
    Therefore, my lords, omit no happy hour
    That may give furth'rance to our expedition:
    For we have now no thought in us but France,
    Save those to God, that run before our business.
    Therefore let our proportions for these wars
    Be soon collected, and all things thought upon
    That may with reasonable swiftness add
    More feathers to our wings: for, God before,
    We'll chide this Dolphin at his father's door.
    Therefore let every man now task his thought,   310
    That this fair action may on foot be brought.

                [Exeunt.

ACT 2. PROLOGUE.

Flourish. Enter CHORUS.

CHORUS   Now all the youth of England are on fire,
And silken dalliance in the wardrobe lies;
Now thrive the armourers, and honour's thought
Reigns solely in the breast of every man.
They sell the pasture now, to buy the horse;
Following the mirror of all Christian kings,
With wingèd heels, as English Mercuries.[19]
For now sits Expectation in the air,
And hides a sword, from hilts unto the point,
With crowns imperial, crowns and coronets,   10
Promised to Harry and his followers.
The French, advised by good intelligence
Of this most dreadful preparation,
Shake in their fear, and with pale policy
Seek to divert the English purposes.
O England: model to thy inward greatness,
Like little body with a mighty heart:
What might'st thou do, that honour would thee do,
Were all thy children kind and natural!
But see, thy fault France hath in thee found out,   20
A nest of hollow bosoms, which he fills
With treacherous crowns; and three corrupted men,
One, Richard Earl of Cambridge, and the second,
Henry Lord Scroop of Masham, and the third,
Sir Thomas Grey, knight of Northumberland,
Have for the gilt of France (O guilt indeed!)
Confirmed conspiracy with fearful France;
And by their hands this grace of kings must die,
If hell and treason hold their promises,
Ere he take ship for France; and in Southampton.   30
Linger your patience on, and we'll digest
Th'abuse of distance, force – perforce – a play.[20]
The sum is paid, the traitors are agreed,
The King is set from London, and the scene

Is now transported, gentles, to Southampton.[21]
There is the playhouse now, there must you sit,
And thence to France shall we convey you safe,
And bring you back, charming the narrow seas
To give you gentle pass: for if we may,
We'll not offend one stomach with our play.   40
But till the King come forth, and not till then,
Unto Southampton do we shift our scene.

[*Exit.*

ACT 2, SCENE I.

London. A street.

Enter Corporal NYM *and Lieutenant* BARDOLPH.

BARDOLPH   Well met, Corporal Nym.

NYM   Good morrow, Lieutenant Bardolph.

BARDOLPH   What, are Ancient Pistol and you friends yet?

NYM   For my part, I care not. I say little; but when time shall
serve, there shall be smiles; but that shall be as it may. I
dare not fight, but I will wink and hold out mine iron:
it is a simple one, but what though? It will toast cheese,
and it will endure cold, as another man's sword will:
and there's an end.

BARDOLPH   I will bestow a breakfast to make you friends, and we'll   10
be all three sworn brothers to France: let't be so, good
Corporal Nym.

NYM   Faith, I will live so long as I may, that's the certain of it;
and when I cannot live any longer, I will do as I may:
that is my rest, that is the rendezvous of it.

BARDOLPH   It is certain, corporal, that he is married to Nell
Quickly; and certainly she did you wrong, for you
were troth-plight to her.

NYM   I cannot tell. Things must be as they may: men may
sleep, and they may have their throats about them at that   20
time, and some say knives have edges. It must be as it
may; though patience be a tired mare, yet she will plod.
There must be conclusions; well, I cannot tell.

Enter PISTOL *and* HOSTESS QUICKLY.

BARDOLPH   Here comes Ancient Pistol and his wife: good corporal,
           be patient here.

NYM   How now, mine host Pistol?

PISTOL   Base tyke, call'st thou me host?
           Now by this hand I swear I scorn the term;
           Nor shall my Nell keep lodgers.

HOSTESS   No, by my troth, not long: for we cannot lodge and   30
           board a dozen or fourteen gentlewomen that live
           honestly by the prick of their needles,[22] but it will be
           thought we keep a bawdy-house straight. [*Nym draws
           his sword; in response, Pistol draws his sword.*] O well-a-
           day, Lady, if he be not hewn now, we shall see wilful
           adultery and murder committed.[23]

BARDOLPH   Good lieutenant, good corporal, offer nothing here.

NYM   Pish!

PISTOL   Pish for thee, Iceland dog! Thou prick-eared cur of
           Iceland![24]   40

HOSTESS   Good Corporal Nym, show thy valour, and put up your
           sword.   [*They sheathe their swords.*

NYM   Will you shog off? I would have you solus.[25]

PISTOL   'Solus', egregious dog? O viper vile!
           The 'solus' in thy most mervailous face,
           The 'solus' in thy teeth, and in thy throat,
           And in thy hateful lungs, yea in thy maw, perdy;
           And, which is worse, within thy nasty mouth!
           I do retort the 'solus' in thy bowels,
           For I can take, and Pistol's cock is up,   50
           And flashing fire will follow.[26]

NYM   I am not Barbason: you cannot conjure me. I have an
           humour to knock you indifferently well. If you grow
           foul with me, Pistol, I will scour you with my rapier, as
           I may, in fair terms. If you would walk off, I would
           prick your guts a little in good terms, as I may, and
           that's the humour of it.

PISTOL   O braggart vile, and damnèd furious wight,
           The grave doth gape, and doting death is near,
           Therefore exhale!   [*They both draw their swords.* 60

BARDOLPH   [*drawing his sword*] Hear me, hear me what I say: he that

strikes the first stroke, I'll run him up to the hilts, as I
am a soldier.

PISTOL   An oath of mickle might, and fury shall abate.

                                        [*They sheathe.*

            Give me thy fist, thy fore-foot to me give:
            Thy spirits are most tall.

NYM   I will cut thy throat one time or other in fair terms;
            that is the humour of it.

PISTOL   'Couple a gorge'![27]
            That is the word. I thee defy again.   70
            O hound of Crete, think'st thou my spouse to get?
            No, to the spital go,
            And from the powdering-tub of infamy
            Fetch forth the lazar kite of Cressid's kind,[28]
            Doll Tearsheet[29] she by name, and her espouse.
            I have, and I will hold, the quondam Quickly[30]
            For the only she: and – pauca, there's enough.
            Go to.

                          Enter the BOY.

BOY   Mine host Pistol, you must come to my master,[31] and
            your hostess: he is very sick, and would to bed. Good 80
            Bardolph, put thy face between his sheets, and do the
            office of a warming-pan: faith, he's very ill.

BARDOLPH   Away, you rogue.   [*Exit Boy.*

HOSTESS   By my troth, he'll yield the crow a pudding one of these
            days. The King has killed his heart.[32] Good husband,
            come home presently.   [*Hostess follows the Boy.*

BARDOLPH   Come, shall I make you two friends? We must to
            France together: why the devil should we keep knives
            to cut one another's throats?

PISTOL   Let floods o'erswell, and fiends for food howl on!   90

NYM   You'll pay me the eight shillings I won of you at
            betting?

PISTOL   Base is the slave that pays.

NYM   That now I will have: that's the humour of it.

PISTOL   As manhood shall compound: push home. [*All draw.*

BARDOLPH   By this sword, he that makes the first thrust, I'll kill
            him; by this sword, I will.

PISTOL   Sword is an oath, and oaths must have their course.

BARDOLPH   Corporal Nym, an thou wilt be friends, be friends; an
            thou wilt not, why then, be enemies with me too. 100
            Prithee put up.

NYM   I shall have my eight shillings I won of you at betting?

PISTOL   A noble shalt thou have, and present pay,
            And liquor likewise will I give to thee,
            And friendship shall combine, and brotherhood.
            I'll live by Nym, and Nym shall live by me.
            Is not this just? For I shall sutler be
            Unto the camp, and profits will accrue. [*They sheathe.*
            Give me thy hand.

NYM   I shall have my noble?   110

PISTOL   In cash, most justly paid.

NYM   Well, then, that's the humour of 't. [*They strike hands.*

Enter HOSTESS.

HOSTESS   As ever you come of women, come in quickly to Sir
            John. Ah, poor heart! He is so shaked of a burning
            quotidian tertian, that it is most lamentable to behold.
            Sweet men, come to him.

NYM   The King hath run bad humours on the knight; that's
            the even of it.

PISTOL   Nym, thou hast spoke the right;
            His heart is fracted and corroborate.   120

NYM   The King is a good king, but it must be as it may; he
            passes some humours and careers.

PISTOL   Let us condole the knight; for (lambkins) we will live.
                                                     [*Exeunt.*

SCENE 2.

Southampton. A council-chamber.

Enter EXETER, BEDFORD, *and* WESTMORLAND.

BEDFORD   'Fore God, his Grace is bold to trust these traitors.

EXETER   They shall be apprehended by and by.

WEST'LAND   How smooth and even they do bear themselves,
            As if allegiance in their bosoms sat,

           Crownèd with faith, and constant loyalty.

BEDFORD   The King hath note of all that they intend,
           By interception which they dream not of.

EXETER   Nay, but the man that was his bedfellow,
           Whom he hath dulled and cloyed with gracious
                                 favours:
           That he should, for a foreign purse, so sell   10
           His sovereign's life to death and treachery!

Sound trumpets. Enter the KING, SCROOP, CAMBRIDGE,
and GREY, *with attendants.*

KING   Now sits the wind fair, and we will aboard.
           My Lord of Cambridge, and my kind Lord of Masham,
           And you, my gentle knight, give me your thoughts:
           Think you not that the powers we bear with us
           Will cut their passage through the force of France,
           Doing the execution and the act
           For which we have in head assembled them?

SCROOP   No doubt, my liege, if each man do his best.

KING   I doubt not that, since we are well persuaded   20
           We carry not a heart with us from hence
           That grows not in a fair consent with ours;
           Nor leave not one behind, that doth not wish
           Success and conquest to attend on us.

CAMB.   Never was monarch better feared and loved
           Than is your Majesty: there's not, I think, a subject
           That sits in heart-grief and uneasiness
           Under the sweet shade of your government.

GREY   True; those that were your father's enemies
           Have steeped their galls in honey, and do serve you   30
           With hearts create of duty and of zeal.

KING   We therefore have great cause of thankfulness,
           And shall forget the office of our hand
           Sooner than quittance of desert and merit,
           According to the weight and worthiness.

SCROOP   So service shall with steelèd sinews toil,
           And labour shall refresh itself with hope
           To do your Grace incessant services.

KING   We judge no less. Uncle of Exeter,

| | Enlarge the man committed yesterday,   40 |

Enlarge the man committed yesterday, 40
That railed against our person: we consider
It was excess of wine that set him on,
And on his more advice we pardon him.

SCROOP   That's mercy, but too much security:
Let him be punished, sovereign, lest example
Breed (by his sufferance) more of such a kind.

KING   O, let us yet be merciful.

CAMB.   So may your Highness, and yet punish too.

GREY   Sir,
You show great mercy if you give him life,   50
After the taste of much correction.

KING   Alas, your too much love and care of me
Are heavy orisons 'gainst this poor wretch.
If little faults, proceeding on distemper,
Shall not be winked at, how shall we stretch our eye
When capital crimes, chewed, swallowed, and digested,
Appear before us? We'll yet enlarge that man,
Though Cambridge, Scroop, and Grey, in their
                                        dear care
And tender preservation of our person
Would have him punished. And now to our
                        French causes: [He takes up papers. 60
Who are the late commissioners?

CAMB.   I one, my lord:
Your Highness bade me ask for it today.

SCROOP   So did you me, my liege.

GREY   And I, my royal sovereign.

KING   [delivering the papers] Then, Richard, Earl of Cambridge,
                                        there is yours;
There yours, Lord Scroop of Masham: and, sir knight,
Grey of Northumberland, this same is yours:
Read them, and know I know your worthiness.
My Lord of Westmorland, and uncle Exeter,   70
We will aboard tonight. – Why, how now, gentlemen?
What see you in those papers, that you lose
So much complexion? – Look ye how they change:
Their cheeks are paper. – Why, what read you there,
That have so cowarded and chased your blood

Out of appearance?

CAMB.   I do confess my fault,
And do submit me to your Highness' mercy.

GREY ⎫
SCROOP ⎭   To which we all appeal.

KING   The mercy that was quick in us but late,
        By your own counsel is suppressed and killed.   80
        You must not dare, for shame, to talk of mercy,
        For your own reasons turn into your bosoms,
        As dogs upon their masters, worrying you.
        See you, my princes, and my noble peers,
        These English monsters! My Lord of Cambridge here,
        You know how apt our love was to accord
        To furnish him with all appertinents
        Belonging to his honour; and this man
        Hath, for a few light crowns, lightly conspired
        And sworn unto the practices of France   90
        To kill us here in Hampton. To the which
        This knight, no less for bounty bound to us
        Than Cambridge is, hath likewise sworn. But O,
        What shall I say to thee, Lord Scroop, thou cruel,
        Ingrateful, savage, and inhuman creature?
        Thou that didst bear the key of all my counsels,
        That knew'st the very bottom of my soul,
        That (almost) mightst have coined me into gold,
        Wouldst thou have practised on me for thy use:
        May it be possible, that foreign hire   100
        Could out of thee extract one spark of evil
        That might annoy my finger? 'Tis so strange,
        That though the truth of it stands off as gross
        As black on white, my eye will scarcely see it.
        Treason and murder ever kept together,
        As two yoke-devils sworn to either's purpose,
        Working so grossly in a natural cause
        That admiration did not whoop at them;[33]
        But thou ('gainst all proportion) didst bring in
        Wonder to wait on treason and on murder;   110
        And whatsoever cunning fiend it was
        That wrought upon thee so preposterously

Hath got the voice in hell for excellence;
All other devils that suggest by treasons
Do botch and bungle up damnation
With patches, colours, and with forms being fetched
From glist'ring semblances of piety;
But he that tempered thee, bade thee stand up,
Gave thee no instance why thou shouldst do treason,
Unless to dub thee with the name of traitor.   120
If that same demon that hath gulled thee thus
Should with his lion-gait walk the whole world,
He might return to vasty Tartar back,
And tell the legions, 'I can never win
A soul so easy as that Englishman's.'
O, how hast thou with jealousy infected
The sweetness of affiance! Show men dutiful?
Why, so didst thou. Seem they grave and learnèd?
Why, so didst thou. Come they of noble family?
Why, so didst thou. Seem they religious?   130
Why, so didst thou. Or are they spare in diet,
Free from gross passion, or of mirth, or anger,
Constant in spirit, not swerving with the blood,
Garnished and decked in modest complement,
Not working with the eye without the ear,
And but in purgèd judgement trusting neither?
Such and so finely bolted didst thou seem:
And thus thy fall hath left a kind of blot,
To mark the full-fraught man and best indued
With some suspicion. I will weep for thee: 140
For this revolt of thine, methinks, is like
Another fall of man.³⁴ Their faults are open;
Arrest them to the answer of the law,
And God acquit them of their practices.

EXETER   I arrest thee of high treason, by the name of Richard
            Earl of Cambridge.
            I arrest thee of high treason, by the name of Henry
            Lord Scroop of Masham.
            I arrest thee of high treason, by the name of Thomas
            Grey, knight of Northumberland.   150

SCROOP   Our purposes God justly hath discovered,

And I repent my fault more than my death;
Which I beseech your Highness to forgive,
Although my body pay the price of it.

CAMB.   For me, the gold of France did not seduce,
Although I did admit it as a motive,
The sooner to effect what I intended;[35]
But God be thankèd for prevention,
Which I in sufferance heartily will rejoice,
Beseeching God, and you, to pardon me.   160

GREY   Never did faithful subject more rejoice
At the discovery of most dangerous treason,
Than I do at this hour joy o'er myself,
Prevented from a damnèd enterprise;
My fault, but not my body, pardon, sovereign.

KING   God quit you in His mercy! Hear your sentence.
You have conspired against our royal person,
Joined with an enemy proclaimed, and from his coffers
Received the golden earnest of our death:
Wherein you would have sold your King to slaughter,   170
His princes and his peers to servitude,
His subjects to oppression and contempt,
And his whole kingdom into desolation.
Touching our person, seek we no revenge;
But we our kingdom's safety must so tender,
Whose ruin you have sought, that to her laws
We do deliver you. Get you therefore hence,
Poor miserable wretches, to your death:
The taste whereof, God of His mercy give
You patience to endure, and true repentance   180
Of all your dear offences. Bear them hence.
    [*Exeunt* CAMBRIDGE, SCROOP, *and* GREY, *guarded.*
Now, lords, for France: the enterprise whereof
Shall be to you as us, like glorious.
We doubt not of a fair and lucky war,
Since God so graciously hath brought to light
This dangerous treason lurking in our way
To hinder our beginnings. We doubt not now
But every rub is smoothèd on our way.
Then forth, dear countrymen: let us deliver

Our puissance into the hand of God,   190
Putting it straight in expedition.
Cheerly to sea, the signs of war advance:
No king of England, if not king of France!

                                    [Flourish. Exeunt.

SCENE 3.

London. Before a tavern.

Enter PISTOL, HOSTESS, NYM, BARDOLPH, *and* BOY.

HOSTESS   Prithee, honey-sweet husband, let me bring thee to
                Staines.

PISTOL   No: for my manly heart doth erne.
                Bardolph, be blithe; Nym, rouse thy vaunting veins;
                Boy, bristle thy courage up: for Falstaff he is dead,
                And we must earn therefore.

BARDOLPH   Would I were with him, wheresome'er he is, either in
                heaven or in hell.

HOSTESS   Nay sure, he's not in hell: he's in Arthur's bosom,[36] if
                ever man went to Arthur's bosom: a made a finer end, 10
                and went away an it had been any christom child. A
                parted even just between twelve and one, even at the
                turning o'th'tide: for after I saw him fumble with the
                sheets, and play with flowers, and smile upon his
                fingers' ends, I knew there was but one way: for his
                nose was as sharp as a pen, and a babbled of green
                fields. 'How now, Sir John?' quoth I. 'What, man! Be
                o' good cheer.' So a cried out, 'God, God, God!' three
                or four times. Now I, to comfort him, bid him a
                should not think of God; I hoped there was no need to 20
                trouble himself with any such thoughts yet. So a bade
                me lay more clothes on his feet. I put my hand into the
                bed, and felt them, and they were as cold as any stone;
                then I felt to his knees, and so upward, and upward,
                and all was as cold as any stone.

NYM   They say he cried out of sack.

HOSTESS   Ay, that a did.

BARDOLPH	And of women.
HOSTESS	Nay, that a did not.
BOY	Yes, that a did, and said they were devils incarnate. 30
HOSTESS	A could never abide carnation; 'twas a colour he never liked.
BOY	A said once, the devil would have him about women.
HOSTESS	A did in some sort (indeed) handle women; but then he was rheumatic, and talked of the Whore of Babylon.37
BOY	Do you not remember a saw a flea stick upon Bardolph's nose, and a said it was a black soul burning in hell?
BARDOLPH	Well, the fuel is gone that maintained that fire: that's all the riches I got in his service. 40
NYM	Shall we shog? The King will be gone from Southampton.
PISTOL	Come, let's away. My love, give me thy lips. Look to my chattels and my movables: Let senses rule: the word is 'Pitch and pay';38 Trust none: For oaths are straws, men's faiths are wafer-cakes, And Holdfast is the only dog, my duck; Therefore, Caveto be thy counsellor.39 Go, clear thy crystals.40 Yoke-fellows in arms, 50 Let us to France, like horse-leeches, my boys, To suck, to suck, the very blood to suck!
BOY	And that's but unwholesome food, they say.
PISTOL	Touch her soft mouth, and march.
BARDOLPH	Farewell, hostess. [He kisses her.
NYM	I cannot kiss, that is the humour of it;41 but adieu.
PISTOL	Let housewifery appear: keep close, I thee command.42
HOSTESS	Farewell; adieu.

[Exeunt.

SCENE 4.

The French King's palace.

Flourish. Enter the FRENCH KING, *the* DOLPHIN, *the Dukes of*
BERRY *and* BRITAINE, *the* CONSTABLE, *and others.*

FR. KING Thus comes the English with full power upon us,
          And more than carefully it us concerns
          To answer royally in our defences.
          Therefore the Dukes of Berry and of Britaine,[43]
          Of Brabant and of Orleance,[44] shall make forth,
          And you, Prince Dolphin, with all swift dispatch
          To line and new repair our towns of war
          With men of courage and with means defendant:
          For England his approaches makes as fierce
          As waters to the sucking of a gulf.   10
          It fits us then to be as provident
          As fear may teach us, out of late examples
          Left by the fatal and neglected English
          Upon our fields.

DOLPHIN   My most redoubted father,
          It is most meet we arm us 'gainst the foe:
          For peace itself should not so dull a kingdom
          (Though war nor no known quarrel were in question)
          But that defences, musters, preparations,
          Should be maintained, assembled, and collected,
          As were a war in expectation.   20
          Therefore I say, 'tis meet we all go forth
          To view the sick and feeble parts of France;
          And let us do it with no show of fear,
          No, with no more than if we heard that England
          Were busied with a Whitsun morris-dance:[45]
          For, my good liege, she is so idly kinged,
          Her sceptre so fantastically borne,
          By a vain, giddy, shallow, humorous youth,
          That fear attends her not.

CONSTABLE   O peace, Prince Dolphin!
          You are too much mistaken in this king: 30

Question your Grace the late ambassadors,
With what great state he heard their embassy,
How well supplied with noble counsellors,
How modest in exception; and, withal,
How terrible in constant resolution:
And you shall find his vanities forespent
Were but the outside of the Roman Brutus,[46]
Covering discretion with a coat of folly;
As gardeners do with ordure hide those roots
That shall first spring, and be most delicate.   40

DOLPHIN Well, 'tis not so, my Lord High Constable.
But though we think it so, it is no matter:
In cases of defence, 'tis best to weigh
The enemy more mighty than he seems,
So the proportions of defence are filled;
Which, of a weak and niggardly projection,
Doth, like a miser, spoil his coat with scanting
A little cloth.

FR. KING   Think we King Harry strong;
And, princes, look you strongly arm to meet him.
The kindred of him hath been fleshed upon us,   50
And he is bred out of that bloody strain
That haunted us in our familiar paths:
Witness our too much memorable shame,
When Cressy battle fatally was struck,
And all our princes captived, by the hand
Of that black name, Edward, Black Prince of Wales;
Whiles that his mountain sire,[47] on mountain standing
Up in the air, crowned with the golden sun,
Saw his heroical seed, and smiled to see him
Mangle the work of nature, and deface   60
The patterns that by God and by French fathers
Had twenty years been made. This is a stem
Of that victorious stock; and let us fear
The native mightiness and fate of him.

Enter a MESSENGER.

MESSENGER Ambassadors from Harry, King of England,
Do crave admittance to your Majesty.

FR. KING   We'll give them present audience. Go, and bring them.
                     [*The Messenger departs with certain lords.*
            You see this chase is hotly followed, friends.
DOLPHIN   Turn head, and stop pursuit: for coward dogs
            Most spend their mouths, when what they seem
                                               to threaten   70
            Runs far before them. Good my sovereign,
            Take up the English short, and let them know
            Of what a monarchy you are the head:
            Self-love, my liege, is not so vile a sin
            As self-neglecting.
                 Re-enter lords, with EXETER *and his train.*

FR. KING   From our brother of England?
EXETER   From him, and thus he greets your Majesty:
            He wills you, in the name of God Almighty,
            That you divest yourself, and lay apart
            The borrowed glories that by gift of heaven,
            By law of nature and of nations, 'longs   80
            To him and to his heirs: namely, the crown,
            And all wide-stretchèd honours that pertain
            By custom, and the ordinance of times,
            Unto the crown of France. That you may know
            'Tis no sinister nor no awkward claim,
            Picked from the worm-holes of long-vanished days,
            Nor from the dust of old oblivion raked,
            He sends you this most memorable line,
                                        [*He gives a paper.*
            In every branch truly demonstrative;
            Willing you overlook this pedigree;   90
            And when you find him evenly derived
            From his most famed of famous ancestors,
            Edward the Third, he bids you then resign
            Your crown and kingdom, indirectly held
            From him, the native and true challenger.
FR. KING   Or else what follows?
EXETER   Bloody constraint: for if you hide the crown
            Even in your hearts, there will he rake for it.
            Therefore in fierce tempest is he coming,
            In thunder and in earthquake, like a Jove:[48] 100

That, if requiring fail, he will compel.
And bids you, in the bowels of the Lord,[49]
Deliver up the crown, and to take mercy
On the poor souls for whom this hungry war
Opens his vasty jaws; and on your head
Turning the widows' tears, the orphans' cries,
The dead men's blood, the pining maidens' groans,
For husbands, fathers, and betrothèd lovers,
That shall be swallowed in this controversy.
This is his claim, his threatening, and my message;   110
Unless the Dolphin be in presence here,
To whom expressly I bring greeting too.

FR. KING   For us, we will consider of this further:
Tomorrow shall you bear our full intent
Back to our brother of England.

DOLPHIN   For the Dolphin,
I stand here for him: what to him from England?

EXETER   Scorn and defiance, slight regard, contempt,
And anything that may not misbecome
The mighty sender, doth he prize you at.
Thus says my King; and if your father's Highness   120
Do not, in grant of all demands at large,
Sweeten the bitter mock you sent his Majesty,
He'll call you to so hot an answer of it
That caves and womby vaultages of France
Shall chide your trespass and return your mock
In second accent of his ordinance.

DOLPHIN   Say: if my father render fair return,
It is against my will: for I desire
Nothing but odds with England. To that end,
As matching to his youth and vanity,   130
I did present him with the Paris-balls.

EXETER   He'll make your Paris Louvre[50] shake for it,
Were it the mistress-court of mighty Europe;
And, be assured, you'll find a difference,
As we his subjects have in wonder found,
Between the promise of his greener days
And these he masters now. Now he weighs time
Even to the utmost grain:[51] that you shall read

In your own losses, if he stay in France.

FR. KING Tomorrow shall you know our mind at full.   140

[*Flourish.*

EXETER Dispatch us with all speed, lest that our King
Come here himself to question our delay;
For he is footed in this land already.

FR. KING You shall be soon dispatched, with fair conditions.
A night is but small breath, and little pause,
To answer matters of this consequence.

[*Exeunt.*

ACT 3. PROLOGUE.

Flourish. Enter CHORUS.

CHORUS   Thus with imagined wing our swift scene flies,
In motion of no less celerity
Than that of thought. Suppose, that you have seen
The well-appointed King at Dover pier[52]
Embark his royalty; and his brave fleet
With silken streamers the young Phoebus fanning.[53]
Play with your fancies: and in them behold,
Upon the hempen tackle, ship-boys climbing;
Hear the shrill whistle, which doth order give
To sounds confused; behold the threaden sails,   10
Borne with th'invisible and creeping wind,
Draw the huge bottoms through the furrowed sea,
Breasting the lofty surge. O, do but think
You stand upon the rivage, and behold
A city on th'inconstant billows dancing:
For so appears this fleet majestical,
Holding due course to Harflew. Follow, follow:
Grapple your minds to sternage of this navy,
And leave your England as dead midnight still,
Guarded with grandsires, babies, and old women,   20
Either past or not arrived to pith and puissance: [54]
For who is he, whose chin is but enriched
With one appearing hair, that will not follow
These culled and choice-drawn cavaliers to France?
Work, work your thoughts, and therein see a siege:
Behold the ordinance on their carriages,
With fatal mouths gaping on girded Harflew.
Suppose th'ambassador from the French comes back:
Tells Harry that the King doth offer him
Katherine his daughter, and with her, to dowry,   30
Some petty and unprofitable dukedoms.
The offer likes not; and the nimble gunner
With linstock now the devilish cannon touches,
                [Alarum, and chambers go off.

And down goes all before them. Still be kind,
And eke out our performance with your mind.

[*Exit.*

ACT 3, SCENE I.

France. Before the gates at Harflew.

Alarum. Enter the KING, EXETER, BEDFORD, *and* GLOUCESTER,
followed by soldiers with scaling ladders.

KING   Once more unto the breach, dear friends, once more;
        Or close the wall up with our English dead!
        In peace, there's nothing so becomes a man
        As modest stillness and humility;
        But when the blast of war blows in our ears,
        Then imitate the action of the tiger:
        Stiffen the sinews, conjure up the blood,
        Disguise fair nature with hard-favoured rage;
        Then lend the eye a terrible aspect:
        Let it pry through the portage of the head,   10
        Like the brass cannon; let the brow o'erwhelm it,
        As fearfully as doth a gallèd rock
        O'erhang and jutty his confounded base,
        Swilled with the wild and wasteful ocean.
        Now set the teeth, and stretch the nostril wide,
        Hold hard the breath, and bend up every spirit
        To his full height. On, on, you noblest English,
        Whose blood is fet from fathers of war-proof:
        Fathers that, like so many Alexanders,[55]
        Have in these parts from morn till even fought,   20
        And sheathed their swords for lack of argument.
        Dishonour not your mothers: now attest
        That those whom you called fathers did beget you.
        Be copy now to men of grosser blood,
        And teach them how to war. And you, good yeomen,
        Whose limbs were made in England, show us here
        The mettle of your pasture;[56] let us swear
        That you are worth your breeding[57] – which I doubt not:

For there is none of you so mean and base,
That hath not noble lustre in your eyes.   30
I see you stand like greyhounds in the slips,
Straining upon the start. The game's afoot:
Follow your spirit; and upon this charge,
Cry, 'God for Harry, England, and Saint George!'[58]

[Exeunt. Alarum, and chambers go off.

SCENE 2.

Enter NYM, BARDOLPH, PISTOL, *and* BOY.

BARDOLPH   On, on, on, on, on! To the breach, to the breach!
NYM   Pray thee, corporal, stay; the knocks are too hot; and for
mine own part, I have not a case of lives. The humour
of it is too hot,[59] that is the very plain-song of it.
PISTOL   The plain-song is most just, for humours do abound.
Knocks go and come; God's vassals drop and die;
          And sword and shield,
          In bloody field,
          Doth win immortal fame.
BOY   Would I were in an alehouse in London! I would give   10
all my fame for a pot of ale, and safety.
PISTOL   And I:
          If wishes would prevail with me,
          My purpose should not fail with me;
          But thither would I hie.
BOY   As duly,
          But not as truly,
          As bird doth sing on bough.

Enter FLUELLEN.

FLUELLEN   Up to the breach, you dogs; avaunt, you cullions!
PISTOL   Be merciful, great duke, to men of mould: 20
Abate thy rage, abate thy manly rage;
Abate thy rage, great duke!
Good bawcock, bate thy rage: use lenity, sweet chuck!
NYM   These be good humours. Your honour wins bad
humours.[60]   *[Exeunt all but Boy.*

BOY   As young as I am, I have observed these three swashers.
           I am boy to them all three, but all they three, though
           they would serve me, could not be man to me; for
           indeed three such antiques do not amount to a man.
           For Bardolph, he is white-livered and red-faced; by   30
           the means whereof, a faces it out, but fights not. For
           Pistol, he hath a killing tongue, and a quiet sword; by
           the means whereof, a breaks words, and keeps whole
           weapons. For Nym, he hath heard that men of few
           words are the best men, and therefore he scorns to say
           his prayers, lest a should be thought a coward: but his
           few bad words are matched with as few good deeds; for
           a never broke any man's head but his own, and that
           was against a post when he was drunk. They will steal
           anything, and call it 'purchase'. Bardolph stole a lute- 40
           case, bore it twelve leagues, and sold it for three
           half-pence. Nym and Bardolph are sworn brothers in
           filching; and in Callice they stole a fire-shovel. I knew
           by that piece of service, the men would carry coals.⁶¹
           They would have me as familiar with men's pockets as
           their gloves or their handkerchers: which makes much
           against my manhood, if I should take from another's
           pocket, to put into mine; for it is plain pocketing-up of
           wrongs. I must leave them, and seek some better
           service: their villany goes against my weak stomach, and 50
           therefore I must cast it up.   [Exit.

                   FLUELLEN returns with GOWER.

GOWER   Captain Fluellen, you must come presently to the
           mines; the Duke of Gloucester would speak with you.
FLUELLEN   To the mines? Tell you the Duke, it is not so good to
           come to the mines: for look you, the mines is not
           according to the disciplines of the war; the concavities of
           it is not sufficient: for look you, th'athversary, you may
           discuss unto the Duke, look you, is digt himself, four
           yard under, the countermines.⁶² By Cheshu, I think a
           will plow up all,⁶³ if there is not better directions.   60
GOWER   The Duke of Gloucester, to whom the order of the
           siege is given, is altogether directed by an Irishman, a
           very valiant gentleman, i'faith.

FLUELLEN   It is Captain Macmorris, is it not?

GOWER   I think it be.

FLUELLEN   By Cheshu, he is an ass, as in the world; I will verify as much in his beard: he has no more directions in the true disciplines of the wars, look you, of the Roman disciplines, than is a puppy-dog.

Enter MACMORRIS *and* CAPTAIN JAMY.

GOWER   Here a comes, and the Scots captain, Captain Jamy, 70 with him.

FLUELLEN   Captain Jamy is a marvellous falorous gentleman, that is certain, and of great expedition and knowledge in th'ancient wars, upon my particular knowledge of his directions: by Cheshu, he will maintain his argument as well as any military man in the world, in the disciplines of the pristine wars of the Romans.

JAMY   I say gud-day, Captain Fluellen.

FLUELLEN   God-den to your worship, good Captain James.

GOWER   How now, Captain Macmorris, have you quit the 80 mines? Have the pioners given o'er?

MACMOR.   By Chrish, law,[64] tish ill done: the work ish give over, the trompet sound the retreat. By my hand I swear, and my father's soul, the work ish ill done: it ish give over; I would have blowed up the town, so Chrish save me, law, in an hour. O tish ill done, tish ill done: by my hand, tish ill done!

FLUELLEN   Captain Macmorris, I beseech you now, will you voutsafe me, look you, a few disputations with you, as partly touching or concerning the disciplines of the 90 war, the Roman wars; in the way of argument, look you, and friendly communication; partly to satisfy my opinion, and partly for the satisfaction, look you, of my mind: as touching the direction of the military discipline, that is the point.

JAMY   It sall be vary gud, gud feith, gud captains bath, and I sall quit you with gud leve,[65] as I may pick occasion; that sall I, marry.

MACMOR.   It is no time to discourse, so Chrish save me: the day is hot, and the weather, and the wars, and the King, and 100

the dukes: it is no time to discourse. The town is
beseeched: and the trumpet call us to the breach, and
we talk, and, be Chrish, do nothing: 'tis shame for us all.
So God sa' me, 'tis shame to stand still, it is shame, by
my hand; and there is throats to be cut, and works to be
done, and there ish nothing done, so Chrish sa' me, law!

JAMY   By the Mess, ere these eyes of mine take themselves to
                slomber, ay'll de gude service, or ay'll lig i'th'grund for
                it. Ay owe God a death,[66] and ay'll pay't as valorously
                as I may, that sal I suerly do, that is the breff and the long. 110
                Mary, I wad full fain heard some question 'tween you
                tway.

FLUELLEN   Captain Macmorris, I think, look you, under your
                correction, there is not many of your nation —

MACMOR.   Of my nation? What ish my nation? Ish a villain, and
                a bastard, and a knave, and a rascal?[67] What ish my
                nation? Who talks of my nation?

FLUELLEN   Look you, if you take the matter otherwise than is
                meant, Captain Macmorris, peradventure I shall think
                you do not use me with that affability as in discretion 120
                you ought to use me, look you, being as good a man as
                yourself, both in the disciplines of war, and in the
                derivation of my birth, and in other particularities.

MACMOR.   I do not know you so good a man as myself: so Chrish
                save me, I will cut off your head.

GOWER   Gentlemen both, you will mistake each other.

JAMY   Ah! That's a foul fault.

                A parley sounded from the walls.

GOWER   The town sounds a parley.

FLUELLEN   Captain Macmorris, when there is more better oppor-
                tunity to be required, look you, I will be so bold as to 130
                tell you I know the disciplines of war; and there is an
                end.

                                                        [*Exeunt.*

SCENE 3.

Some CITIZENS *appear upon the walls.*
Enter the KING *and all his train before the gates*

KING   How yet resolves the Governor of the town?
This is the latest parle we will admit;
Therefore to our best mercy give yourselves,
Or, like to men proud of destruction,
Defy us to our worst; for, as I am a soldier,
A name that in my thoughts becomes me best,
If I begin the battery once again,
I will not leave the half-achieved Harflew
Till in her ashes she lie burièd.
The gates of mercy shall be all shut up,   10
And the fleshed soldier, rough and hard of heart,
In liberty of bloody hand, shall range
With conscience wide as hell, mowing like grass
Your fresh fair virgins and your flowering infants.
What is it then to me, if impious War,
Arrayed in flames like to the Prince of Fiends,
Do with his smirched complexion all fell feats
Enlinked to waste and desolation?
What is't to me, when you yourselves are cause,
If your pure maidens fall into the hand   20
Of hot and forcing violation?
What rein can hold licentious wickedness,
When down the hill he holds his fierce career?
We may as bootless spend our vain command
Upon th'enragèd soldiers in their spoil,
As send precepts to the leviathan
To come ashore.[68] Therefore, you men of Harflew,
Take pity of your town and of your people,
Whiles yet my soldiers are in my command;
Whiles yet the cool and temperate wind of grace 30
O'erblows the filthy and contagious clouds
Of heady murder, spoil, and villainy.
If not: why, in a moment look to see
The blind and bloody soldier with foul hand

Defile the locks of your shrill-shrieking daughters;
Your fathers taken by the silver beards,
And their most reverend heads dashed to the walls;
Your naked infants spitted upon pikes,
Whiles the mad mothers with their howls confused
Do break the clouds, as did the wives of Jewry   40
At Herod's bloody-hunting slaughtermen.[69]
What say you? Will you yield, and this avoid?
Or, guilty in defence, be thus destroyed?

Enter GOVERNOR *on the wall.*

GOVERNOR Our expectation hath this day an end:
The Dolphin, whom of succours we entreated,
Returns us that his powers are yet not ready
To raise so great a siege. Therefore, great King,
We yield our town and lives to thy soft mercy:
Enter our gates, dispose of us and ours,
For we no longer are defensible.   50
KING Open your gates. Come, uncle Exeter,
Go you and enter Harflew; there remain,
And fortify it strongly 'gainst the French.
Use mercy to them all for us, dear uncle.[70]
The winter coming on, and sickness growing
Upon our soldiers, we will retire to Callice.
Tonight in Harflew will we be your guest;
Tomorrow for the march are we addrest.

[*Flourish. The King and his forces enter the town.*

SCENE 4.[71]

Rouen. The French King's palace.

The Princess KATHERINE *and* ALICE, *an old Gentlewoman.*

KATHERINE Alice, tu as été en Angleterre, et tu bien parles le langage.[72]
ALICE Un peu, madame.
KATHERINE Je te prie, m'enseignez:[73] il faut que j'apprenne à parler.
Comment appelez-vous la main en anglais?
ALICE La main? Elle est appelée de hand.
KATHERINE De hand. Et les doigts?

ALICE	Les doigts? Ma foi, j'oublie les doigts; mais je me souviendrai. Les doigts? Je pense qu'ils sont appelés de fingres; oui, de fingres.
KATHERINE	La main, de hand; les doigts, de fingres. Je pense que je suis le bon écolier.[74] J'ai gagné deux mots d'anglais vitement. Comment appelez-vous les ongles?
ALICE	Les ongles? Nous les appelons de nails.
KATHERINE	De nails. Ecoutez: dites-moi si je parle bien: de hand, de fingres, et de nails.
ALICE	C'est bien dit, madame; il est fort bon anglais.[75]
KATHERINE	Dites-moi l'anglais pour le bras.
ALICE	De arm, madame.
KATHERINE	Et le coude.
ALICE	D'elbow.
KATHERINE	D'elbow. Je m'en fais la répétition[76] de tous les mots que vous m'avez appris dès à présent.
ALICE	Il est trop difficile, madame, comme je pense.
KATHERINE	Excusez-moi, Alice; écoutez: d'hand, de fingre, de nails, d'arma, de bilbow.
ALICE	D'elbow, madame.
KATHERINE	O Seigneur Dieu, je m'en oublie![77] D'elbow. Comment appelez-vous le col?
ALICE	De nick, madame.
KATHERINE	De nick. Et le menton?
ALICE	De chin.
KATHERINE	De sin. Le col, de nick; le menton, de sin.
ALICE	Oui. Sauf votre honneur, en vérité, vous prononcez les mots aussi droit[78] que les natifs d'Angleterre.
KATHERINE	Je ne doute point d'apprendre, par la grâce de Dieu, et en peu de temps.
ALICE	N'avez-vous pas déjà oublié ce que je vous ai enseigné?
KATHERINE	Non, je réciterai à vous[79] promptement: d'hand, de fingre, de mailès —
ALICE	De nails, madame.
KATHERINE	De nails, de arm, de ilbow.
ALICE	Sauf votre honneur, d'elbow.
KATHERINE	Ainsi dis-je: d'elbow, de nick, et de sin. Comment appelez-vous le pied et la robe?
ALICE	Le foot, madame, et le coun.

10

20

30

40

KATHERINE   Le foot, et le coun?[80] O Seigneur Dieu! Ils sont mots[81]
de son mauvais, corruptible, gros et impudique, et non
pour les dames d'honneur d'user:[82] je ne voudrais
prononcer ces mots devant les seigneurs de France pour
tout le monde. Foh! Le foot et le coun! Néanmoins, je   50
réciterai une autre fois[83] ma leçon ensemble: d'hand, de
fingre, de nails, d'arm, d'elbow, de nick, de sin, de foot,
le coun.

ALICE   Excellent, madame!

KATHERINE   C'est assez pour une fois: allons-nous à dîner.[84]

                                                    [*Exeunt.*

SCENE 5.

Enter the KING *of France, the* DOLPHIN, *the* DUKE OF BRITAINE,
the CONSTABLE *of France, and others.*

FR. KING   'Tis certain he hath passed the river Somme.

CONSTABLE   And if he be not fought withal, my lord,
Let us not live in France: let us quit all,
And give our vineyards to a barbarous people.

DOLPHIN   O Dieu vivant![85] Shall a few sprays of us,
The emptying of our fathers' luxury,
Our scions, put in wild and savage stock,
Spirt up so suddenly into the clouds,
And overlook their grafters?[86]

BRITAINE   Normans, but bastard Normans, Norman bastards!   10
Mort de ma vie![87] If they march along
Unfought withal, but I will sell my dukedom
To buy a slobbery and a dirty farm
In that nook-shotten isle of Albion.

CONSTABLE   Dieu de batailles![88] Where have they this mettle?
Is not their climate foggy, raw, and dull?
On whom, as in despite, the sun looks pale,
Killing their fruit with frowns. Can sodden water,
A drench for sur-reined jades, their barley broth,
Decoct their cold blood to such valiant heat?   20
And shall our quick blood, spirited with wine,
Seem frosty? O, for honour of our land,
Let us not hang like roping icicles

Upon our houses' thatch, whiles a more frosty people
Sweat drops of gallant youth in our rich fields![89] –
Poor may we call them in their native lords.[90]

DOLPHIN   By faith and honour,
Our madams mock at us, and plainly say
Our mettle is bred out, and they will give
Their bodies to the lust of English youth,   30
To new-store France with bastard warriors.

BRITAINE   They bid us to the English dancing-schools,
And teach lavoltas high, and swift corantos,
Saying our grace is only in our heels,
And that we are most lofty runaways.

FR. KING   Where is Montjoy the herald? Speed him hence:
Let him greet England with our sharp defiance.
Up, princes, and with spirit of honour edged
More sharper than your swords, hie to the field.
Charles Delabreth, High Constable of France,   40
You Dukes of Orleance, Bourbon, and of Berry,
Alanson, Brabant, Bar, and Burgundy,
Jacques Chatillion, Rambures, Vaudemont,
Beaumont, Grandpré, Roussi, and Faulconbridge,
Foix, Lestrale, Bouciqualt, and Charolois,
High dukes, great princes, barons, lords, and knights:
For your great seats now quit you of great shames.
Bar Harry England, that sweeps through our land
With pennons painted in the blood of Harflew:
Rush on his host, as doth the melted snow   50
Upon the valleys, whose low vassal seat
The Alps doth spit and void his rheum[91] upon.
Go down upon him, you have power enough;
And in a captive chariot[92] into Roan
Bring him our prisoner.

CONSTABLE   This becomes the great.
Sorry am I his numbers are so few,
His soldiers sick and famished in their march:
For I am sure, when he shall see our army,
He'll drop his heart into the sink of fear,
And for achievement offer us his ransom.   60

FR. KING   Therefore, Lord Constable, haste on Montjoy,

And let him say to England, that we send
To know what willing ransom he will give.
Prince Dolphin, you shall stay with us in Roan.

DOLPHIN   Not so, I do beseech your majesty.

FR. KING   Be patient, for you shall remain with us.
Now forth, Lord Constable and princes all,
And quickly bring us word of England's fall.

[*Exeunt.*

SCENE 6.

The English camp in Picardy.

Enter the English and Welsh Captains, GOWER *and* FLUELLEN.

GOWER   How now, Captain Fluellen! Come you from the
bridge?

FLUELLEN   I assure you, there is very excellent services committed
at the bridge.[93]

GOWER   Is the Duke of Exeter safe?

FLUELLEN   The Duke of Exeter is as magnanimous as Agamemnon,[94] and a man that I love and honour with my soul,
and my heart, and my duty, and my live, and my
living, and my uttermost power. He is not – God be
praised and blessed! – any hurt in the world, but keeps   10
the bridge most valiantly, with excellent discipline.
There is an ancient lieutenant there at the pridge, I
think in my very conscience he is as valiant a man as
Mark Antony,[95] and he is a man of no estimation in the
world, but I did see him do as gallant service.

GOWER   What do you call him?

FLUELLEN   He is called Ancient Pistol.

GOWER   I know him not.

Enter PISTOL.

FLUELLEN   Here is the man.

PISTOL   Captain, I thee beseech to do me favours: 20
The Duke of Exeter doth love thee well.

FLUELLEN   Ay, I praise God, and I have merited some love at his
hands.

PISTOL   Bardolph, a soldier firm and sound of heart,
And of buxom valour, hath, by cruel fate,
And giddy Fortune's furious fickle wheel,
That goddess blind,
That stands upon the rolling restless stone –

FLUELLEN   By your patience, Ancient Pistol: Fortune is painted
blind, with a muffler afore her eyes, to signify to you that   30
Fortune is blind; and she is painted also with a wheel, to
signify to you, which is the moral of it, that she is
turning and inconstant, and mutability, and variation;
and her foot, look you, is fixed upon a spherical stone,
which rolls, and rolls, and rolls: in good truth, the poet
makes a most excellent description of it: Fortune is an
excellent moral.

PISTOL   Fortune is Bardolph's foe, and frowns on him:
For he hath stolen a pax,[96] and hangèd must a be –
A damnèd death!   40
Let gallows gape for dog, let man go free,
And let not hemp his windpipe suffocate.
But Exeter hath given the doom of death
For pax of little price.
Therefore go speak, the Duke will hear thy voice;
And let not Bardolph's vital thread be cut
With edge of penny cord, and vile reproach.
Speak, captain, for his life, and I will thee requite.

FLUELLEN   Ancient Pistol, I do partly understand your meaning.

PISTOL   Why then, rejoice therefore.   50

FLUELLEN   Certainly, ancient, it is not a thing to rejoice at: for if,
look you, he were my brother, I would desire the
Duke to use his good pleasure, and put him to execu-
tion; for discipline ought to be used.

PISTOL   Die and be damned! And figo for thy friendship!

FLUELLEN   It is well.

PISTOL   The fig of Spain!   [Exit.

FLUELLEN   Very good.

GOWER   Why, this is an arrant counterfeit rascal: I remember
him now: a bawd, a cutpurse.   60

FLUELLEN   I'll assure you, a uttered as prave words at the pridge as
you shall see in a summer's day; but it is very well,

what he has spoke to me; that is well, I warrant you,
when time is serve.

GOWER　　Why, 'tis a gull, a fool, a rogue, that now and then goes
to the wars, to grace himself at his return into London,
under the form of a soldier. And such fellows are perfect
in the great commanders' names, and they will learn
you by rote where services were done: at such and such
a sconce, at such a breach, at such a convoy; who came　70
off bravely, who was shot, who disgraced, what terms
the enemy stood on; and this they con perfectly in the
phrase of war, which they trick up with new-tuned
oaths; and what a beard of the general's cut, and a horrid
suit of the camp, will do among foaming bottles, and
ale-washed wits, is wonderful to be thought on. But
you must learn to know such slanders of the age, or else
you may be marvellously mistook.

FLUELLEN　I tell you what, Captain Gower: I do perceive he is not
the man that he would gladly make show to the world　80
he is. If I find a hole in his coat,[97] I will tell him my
mind. [Drum heard.] Hark you, the King is coming,
and I must speak with him from the pridge.

Drum and colours. Enter the KING, *his poor soldiers,*
and GLOUCESTER.

FLUELLEN　God pless your Majesty!
KING　　　How now, Fluellen, cam'st thou from the bridge?
FLUELLEN　Ay, so please your Majesty. The Duke of Exeter has
very gallantly maintained the pridge; the French is gone
off, look you, and there is gallant and most prave
passages. Marry, th'athversary was have possession of
the pridge, but he is enforced to retire, and the Duke of　90
Exeter is master of the pridge. I can tell your Majesty,
the Duke is a prave man.

KING　　　What men have you lost, Fluellen?
FLUELLEN　The perdition of th'athversary hath been very great,
reasonable great. Marry, for my part, I think the Duke
hath lost never a man, but one that is like to be
executed for robbing a church, one Bardolph, if your
Majesty know the man: his face is all bubukles and

whelks,[98] and knobs, and flames o' fire, and his lips
blows at his nose, and it is like a coal of fire, sometimes   100
plue, and sometimes red; but his nose is executed, and
his fire's out.

KING   We would have all such offenders so cut off; and we
            give express charge that in our marches through the
            country, there be nothing compelled from the villages;
            nothing taken but paid for; none of the French up-
            braided or abused in disdainful language; for when
            lenity and cruelty play for a kingdom, the gentler
            gamester is the soonest winner.

                        Tucket. Enter MONTJOY.

MONTJOY   You know me by my habit.   110
KING   Well then, I know thee: what shall I know of thee?
MONTJOY   My master's mind.
KING   Unfold it.
MONTJOY   Thus says my King: 'Say thou to Harry of England,
            though we seemed dead, we did but sleep: advantage
            is a better soldier than rashness. Tell him, we could
            have rebuked him at Harflew, but that we thought
            not good to bruise an injury till it were full ripe. Now
            we speak upon our cue, and our voice is imperial:
            England shall repent his folly, see his weakness, and   120
            admire our sufferance.[99] Bid him therefore consider of
            his ransom, which must proportion the losses we have
            borne, the subjects we have lost, the disgrace we have
            digested; which in weight to re-answer, his pettiness
            would bow under. For our losses, his exchequer is too
            poor; for th'effusion of our blood, the muster of his
            kingdom too faint a number; and for our disgrace, his
            own person, kneeling at our feet, but a weak and
            worthless satisfaction. To this add defiance; and tell
            him, for conclusion, he hath betrayed his followers,   130
            whose condemnation is pronounced.' So far my King
            and master; so much my office.
KING   What is thy name? I know thy quality.
MONTJOY   Montjoy.
KING   Thou dost thy office fairly. Turn thee back,
            And tell thy King I do not seek him now,

But could be willing to march on to Callice
Without impeachment: for, to say the sooth,
Though 'tis no wisdom to confess so much
Unto an enemy of craft and vantage,   140
My people are with sickness much enfeebled,
My numbers lessened; and those few I have,
Almost no better than so many French;
Who when they were in health, I tell thee, herald,
I thought upon one pair of English legs
Did march three Frenchmen. Yet forgive me, God,
That I do brag thus; this your air of France
Hath blown that vice in me. I must repent.
Go therefore, tell thy master, here I am;
My ransom is this frail and worthless trunk;   150
My army, but a weak and sickly guard;
Yet, God before, tell him we will come on,
Though France himself, and such another neighbour,
Stand in our way. There's for thy labour, Montjoy.[100]
                              [*Montjoy receives gift.*
Go bid thy master well advise himself.
If we may pass, we will; if we be hindered,
We shall your tawny ground with your red blood
Discolour: and so, Montjoy, fare you well.
The sum of all our answer is but this:
We would not seek a battle as we are,   160
Nor, as we are, we say we will not shun it.
So tell your master.
MONTJOY   I shall deliver so. Thanks to your Highness.
                                        [*Exit.*

GLO'STER   I hope they will not come upon us now.
KING   We are in God's hand, brother, not in theirs.
            March to the bridge; it now draws toward night:
            Beyond the river we'll encamp ourselves,
            And on tomorrow bid them march away.
                                        [*Exeunt.*

SCENE 7.

The French camp, near Agincourt.

Enter the CONSTABLE OF FRANCE, *the Lord* RAMBURES,
ORLEANCE, DOLPHIN, *with others.*

CONSTABLE   Tut! I have the best armour of the world. Would it
were day!

ORLEANCE   You have an excellent armour; but let my horse have
his due.

CONSTABLE   It is the best horse of Europe.

ORLEANCE   Will it never be morning?

DOLPHIN   My Lord of Orleance, and my Lord High Constable,
you talk of horse and armour?

ORLEANCE   You are as well provided of both as any prince in the
world.   10

DOLPHIN   What a long night is this! I will not change my horse
with any that treads but on four pasterns. Ça,[101] ha! He
bounds from the earth, as if his entrails were hairs:[102] le
cheval volant, the Pegasus, qui a les narines de feu.[103]
When I bestride him, I soar, I am a hawk: he trots the
air; the earth sings when he touches it: the basest horn
of his hoof is more musical than the pipe of Hermes.[104]

ORLEANCE   He's of the colour of the nutmeg.

DOLPHIN   And of the heat of the ginger. It is a beast for Perseus:[105]
he is pure air and fire; and the dull elements of earth   20
and water never appear in him,[106] but only in patient
stillness while his rider mounts him. He is indeed a
horse, and all other jades you may call beasts.

CONSTABLE   Indeed, my lord, it is a most absolute and excellent
horse.

DOLPHIN   It is the prince of palfreys: his neigh is like the bidding
of a monarch, and his countenance enforces homage.

ORLEANCE   No more, cousin.

DOLPHIN   Nay, the man hath no wit that cannot, from the rising
of the lark to the lodging of the lamb, vary deserved   30
praise on my palfrey: it is a theme as fluent as the sea:
turn the sands into eloquent tongues, and my horse is

argument for them all: 'tis a subject for a sovereign to reason on, and for a sovereign's sovereign to ride on, and for the world, familiar to us and unknown, to lay apart their particular functions and wonder at him. I once writ a sonnet in his praise, and began thus, 'Wonder of nature'.

ORLEANCE I have heard a sonnet begin so to one's mistress.

DOLPHIN Then did they imitate that which I composed to my 40 courser, for my horse is my mistress.

ORLEANCE Your mistress bears well.

DOLPHIN *Me* well, which is the prescript praise and perfection of a good and particular mistress.

CONSTABLE Nay, for methought yesterday your mistress shrewdly shook your back.

DOLPHIN So perhaps did yours.

CONSTABLE Mine was not bridled.

DOLPHIN O then belike she was old and gentle, and you rode like a kern of Ireland, your French hose off, and in 50 your strait strossers.[107]

CONSTABLE You have good judgement in horsemanship.

DOLPHIN Be warned by me then: they that ride so, and ride not warily, fall into foul bogs.[108] I had rather have my horse to my mistress.

CONSTABLE I had as lief have my mistress a jade.

DOLPHIN I tell thee, Constable, my mistress wears his own hair.

CONSTABLE I could make as true a boast as that, if I had a sow to my mistress.

DOLPHIN 'Le chien est retourné à son propre vomissement, et la 60 truie lavée au bourbier':[109] thou makest use of anything.

CONSTABLE Yet do I not use my horse for my mistress, or any such proverb so little kin to the purpose.

RAMBURES My Lord Constable, the armour that I saw in your tent tonight: are those stars or suns upon it?

CONSTABLE Stars, my lord.

DOLPHIN Some of them will fall tomorrow, I hope.

CONSTABLE And yet my sky shall not want.

DOLPHIN That may be, for you bear a many superfluously, and 'twere more honour some were away.   70

CONSTABLE   Ev'n as your horse bears your praises, who would trot
             as well, were some of your brags dismounted.

DOLPHIN   Would I were able to load him with his desert! Will it
             never be day? I will trot tomorrow a mile, and my way
             shall be paved with English faces.

CONSTABLE   I will not say so, for fear I should be faced out of my
             way; but I would it were morning, for I would fain be
             about the ears of the English.

RAMBURES   Who will go to hazard with me for twenty prisoners?

CONSTABLE   You must first go yourself to hazard, ere you have them. 80

DOLPHIN   'Tis midnight, I'll go arm myself.   [Exit.

ORLEANCE   The Dolphin longs for morning.

RAMBURES   He longs to eat the English.

CONSTABLE   I think he will eat all he kills.

ORLEANCE   By the white hand of my lady, he's a gallant prince.

CONSTABLE   Swear by her foot, that she may tread out the oath.[110]

ORLEANCE   He is simply the most active gentleman of France.

CONSTABLE   Doing is activity, and he will still be doing.[111]

ORLEANCE   He never did harm, that I heard of.

CONSTABLE   Nor will do none tomorrow: he will keep that good 90
             name still.

ORLEANCE   I know him to be valiant.

CONSTABLE   I was told that, by one that knows him better than you.

ORLEANCE   What's he?

CONSTABLE   Marry, he told me so himself, and he said he cared not
             who knew it.

ORLEANCE   He needs not, it is no hidden virtue in him.

CONSTABLE   By my faith, sir, but it is: never anybody saw it, but his
             lackey: 'tis a hooded valour, and when it appears, it
             will bate.[112]   100

ORLEANCE   'Ill will never said well.'

CONSTABLE   I will cap that proverb with 'There is flattery in friend-
             ship.'

ORLEANCE   And I will take up that with 'Give the devil his due.'

CONSTABLE   Well placed: there stands your friend for the devil.
             Have at the very eye of that proverb with 'A pox of the
             devil.'

ORLEANCE   You are the better at proverbs, by how much 'A fool's
             bolt is soon shot.'

CONSTABLE You have shot over.   110
ORLEANCE 'Tis not the first time you were overshot.[113]

Enter a MESSENGER.

MESSENGER My Lord High Constable, the English lie within fifteen
hundred paces of your tents.
CONSTABLE Who hath measured the ground?
MESSENGER The Lord Grandpré.
CONSTABLE A valiant and most expert gentleman. Would it were
day! Alas, poor Harry of England! He longs not for the
dawning, as we do.
ORLEANCE What a wretched and peevish fellow is this King of
England, to mope with his fat-brained followers so far   120
out of his knowledge![114]
CONSTABLE If the English had any apprehension, they would run
away.
ORLEANCE That they lack: for if their heads had any intellectual
armour, they could never wear such heavy head-
pieces.
RAMBURES That island of England breeds very valiant creatures;
their mastiffs are of unmatchable courage.
ORLEANCE Foolish curs, that run winking into the mouth of a
Russian bear,[115] and have their heads crushed like rotten   130
apples. You may as well say, that's a valiant flea that
dare eat his breakfast on the lip of a lion.
CONSTABLE Just, just; and the men do sympathise with the mastiffs
in robustious and rough coming on, leaving their wits
with their wives; and then, give them great meals of
beef, and iron and steel, they will eat like wolves and
fight like devils.
ORLEANCE Ay, but these English are shrewdly out of beef.
CONSTABLE Then shall we find tomorrow they have only stomachs
to eat, and none to fight. Now is it time to arm: come,   140
shall we about it?
ORLEANCE It is now two o'clock; but, let me see, by ten
We shall have each a hundred Englishmen.

[*Exeunt.*

ACT 4. PROLOGUE.

Enter CHORUS.

CHORUS   Now entertain conjecture of a time
When creeping murmur and the poring dark
Fills the wide vessel of the universe.
From camp to camp, through the foul womb of night
The hum of either army stilly sounds,
That the fixed sentinels almost receive
The secret whispers of each other's watch.
Fire answers fire, and through their paly flames
Each battle sees the other's umbered face.
Steed threatens steed, in high and boastful neighs   10
Piercing the night's dull ear; and from the tents
The armourers, accomplishing the knights,
With busy hammers closing rivets up,
Give dreadful note of preparation.
The country cocks do crow, the clocks do toll,
And the third hour of drowsy morning name.
Proud of their numbers, and secure in soul,
The confident and over-lusty French
Do the low-rated English play at dice,
And chide the cripple tardy-gaited night,   20
Who like a foul and ugly witch doth limp
So tediously away. The poor condemned English,
Like sacrifices, by their watchful fires
Sit patiently, and inly ruminate
The morning's danger; and their gesture sad,
Investing lank-lean cheeks and war-worn coats,
Presenteth them unto the gazing moon
So many horrid ghosts. O now, who will behold
The royal captain of this ruined band
Walking from watch to watch, from tent to tent,   30
Let him cry, 'Praise and glory on his head!':
For forth he goes, and visits all his host,
Bids them good morrow with a modest smile,
And calls them brothers, friends, and countrymen.
Upon his royal face there is no note

How dread an army hath enrounded him;
Nor doth he dedicate one jot of colour
Unto the weary and all-watched night;
But freshly looks, and over-bears attaint
With cheerful semblance[116] and sweet majesty: 40
That every wretch, pining and pale before,
Beholding him, plucks comfort from his looks.
A largess universal, like the sun,
His liberal eye doth give to every one,
Thawing cold fear, that mean and gentle all
Behold, as may unworthiness define,
A little touch of Harry in the night.
And so our scene must to the battle fly:
Where – O for pity! – we shall much disgrace,
With four or five most vile and ragged foils   50
(Right ill-disposed, in brawl ridiculous),
The name of Agincourt: yet sit and see,
Minding true things by what their mock'ries be.

                                                          [*Exit.*

ACT 4, SCENE I.

The English camp at Agincourt.

Ennter KING HENRY, BEDFORD, *and* GLOUCESTER.

KING   Gloucester, 'tis true that we are in great danger;
              The greater therefore should our courage be.
              Good morrow, brother Bedford. God Almighty!
              There is some soul of goodness in things evil,
              Would men observingly distil it out:
              For our bad neighbour makes us early stirrers,
              Which is both healthful and good husbandry.
              Besides, they are our outward consciences
              And preachers to us all, admonishing
              That we should dress us fairly for our end.   10
              Thus may we gather honey from the weed,
              And make a moral of[117] the devil himself.

                         Enter ERPINGHAM.

              Good morrow, old Sir Thomas Erpingham.

A good soft pillow for that good white head
Were better than a churlish turf of France.

ERPING.   Not so, my liege: this lodging likes me better,
Since I may say 'Now lie I like a king.'

KING   'Tis good for men to love their present pains
Upon example:[118] so the spirit is eased;
And when the mind is quickened, out of doubt   20
The organs, though defunct and dead before,
Break up their drowsy grave, and newly move
With casted slough and fresh legerity.
Lend me thy cloak, Sir Thomas. Brothers both,
Commend me to the princes in our camp;
Do my good morrow to them, and anon
Desire them all to my pavilion.

GLOSTER   We shall, my liege.

ERPING.   Shall I attend your Grace?

KING   No, my good knight:
Go with my brothers to my lords of England.   30
I and my bosom must debate awhile,
And then I would no other company.

ERPING.   The Lord in heaven bless thee, noble Harry!

KING   God-a-mercy, old heart; thou speak'st cheerfully.

                                  [*Exeunt all but the King.*

                              Enter PISTOL.

PISTOL   Qui vous là?[119]
KING   A friend.
PISTOL   Discuss unto me: art thou officer,
Or art thou base, common, and popular?
KING   I am a gentleman of a company.
PISTOL   Trail'st thou the puissant pike?   40
KING   Even so. What are you?
PISTOL   As good a gentleman as the Emperor.[120]
KING   Then you are a better than the King.
PISTOL   The King's a bawcock, and a heart of gold,
A lad of life, an imp of fame,
Of parents good, of fist most valiant:
I kiss his dirty shoe, and from heart-string
I love the lovely bully. What is thy name?

KING	Harry le Roy.[121]
PISTOL	Le Roy? A Cornish name: art thou of Cornish crew? 50
KING	No, I am a Welshman.[122]
PISTOL	Know'st thou Fluellen?
KING	Yes.
PISTOL	Tell him I'll knock his leek about his pate Upon Saint Davy's day.[123]
KING	Do not you wear your dagger in your cap that day, lest he knock that about yours.
PISTOL	Art thou his friend?
KING	And his kinsman too.
PISTOL	The figo for thee then! 60
KING	I thank you: God be with you.
PISTOL	My name is Pistol called. [*Exit.*
KING	It sorts well with your fierceness.

Enter FLUELLEN *and* GOWER.

GOWER	Captain Fluellen!
FLUELLEN	So! In the name of Jesu Christ, speak fewer. It is the greatest admiration in the universal world, when the true and ancient prerogatifes and laws of the wars is not kept. If you would take the pains but to examine the wars of Pompey the Great, you shall find, I warrant you, that there is no tiddle taddle nor pibble pabble in 70 Pompey's camp: I warrant you, you shall find the ceremonies of the wars, and the cares of it, and the forms of it, and the sobriety of it, and the modesty of it, to be otherwise.
GOWER	Why, the enemy is loud; you hear him all night.
FLUELLEN	If the enemy is an ass and a fool, and a prating coxcomb, is it meet, think you, that we should also, look you, be an ass and a fool, and a prating coxcomb? In your own conscience now?
GOWER	I will speak lower. 80
FLUELLEN	I pray you, and beseech you, that you will.
	[*Exeunt Gower and Fluellen.*
KING	Though it appear a little out of fashion, There is much care and valour in this Welshman.

Enter three soldiers, JOHN BATES, ALEXANDER COURT, *and* MICHAEL WILLIAMS.

COURT   Brother John Bates, is not that the morning which breaks yonder?

BATES   I think it be; but we have no great cause to desire the approach of day.

WILLIAMS We see yonder the beginning of the day, but I think we shall never see the end of it. Who goes there?

KING   A friend.   90

WILLIAMS Under what captain serve you?

KING   Under Sir Thomas Erpingham.

WILLIAMS A good old commander, and a most kind gentleman. I pray you, what thinks he of our estate?

KING   Even as men wracked upon a sand, that look to be washed off the next tide.

BATES   He hath not told his thought to the King?

KING   No; nor it is not meet he should: for, though I speak it to you, I think the King is but a man, as I am: the violet smells to him as it doth to me; the element shows to 100 him as it doth to me; all his senses have but human conditions. His ceremonies laid by, in his nakedness he appears but a man; and though his affections are higher mounted than ours, yet, when they stoop, they stoop with the like wing.[124] Therefore, when he sees reason of fears, as we do, his fears, out of doubt, be of the same relish as ours are; yet, in reason, no man should possess him with any appearance of fear, lest he, by showing it, should dishearten his army.

BATES   He may show what outward courage he will; but I 110 believe, as cold a night as 'tis, he could wish himself in Thames up to the neck; and so I would he were, and I by him, at all adventures, so we were quit here.

KING   By my troth, I will speak my conscience of the King: I think he would not wish himself anywhere but where he is.

BATES   Then I would he were here alone: so should he be sure to be ransomed, and a many poor men's lives saved.

KING   I dare say you love him not so ill, to wish him here alone, howsoever you speak this to feel other men's 120

minds. Methinks I could not die anywhere so con-
tented as in the King's company; his cause being just,
and his quarrel honourable.

WILLIAMS That's more than we know.

BATES Ay, or more than we should seek after; for we know
enough, if we know we are the King's subjects: if his
cause be wrong, our obedience to the King wipes the
crime of it out of us.

WILLIAMS But if the cause be not good, the King himself hath a
heavy reckoning to make, when all those legs, and 130
arms, and heads, chopped off in a battle, shall join
together at the latter day,[125] and cry all: 'We died at such
a place; some swearing, some crying for a surgeon;
some upon their wives, left poor behind them; some
upon the debts they owe; some upon their children
rawly left.' I am afeard there are few die well, that die
in a battle: for how can they charitably dispose of
anything, when blood is their argument? Now, if these
men do not die well, it will be a black matter for the
King, that led them to it; who to disobey were against 140
all proportion of subjection.[126]

KING So, if a son that is by his father sent about merchandise
do sinfully miscarry upon the sea, the imputation of his
wickedness, by your rule, should be imposed upon his
father that sent him; or if a servant, under his master's
command, transporting a sum of money, be assailed by
robbers, and die in many irreconciled iniquities, you
may call the business of the master the author of the
servant's damnation. But this is not so. The King is not
bound to answer the particular endings of his soldiers, 150
the father of his son, nor the master of his servant: for
they purpose not their death, when they purpose their
services. Besides, there is no king, be his cause never so
spotless, if it come to the arbitrement of swords, can try
it out with all unspotted soldiers. Some (peradventure)
have on them the guilt of premeditated and contrived
murder; some, of beguiling virgins with the broken
seals of perjury; some, making the wars their bulwark,
that have before gored the gentle bosom of peace with

pillage and robbery. Now, if these men have defeated 160
the law and outrun native punishment, though they
can outstrip men, they have no wings to fly from God.
War is His beadle, war is His vengeance: so that here
men are punished, for before breach of the King's laws,
in now the King's quarrel: where they feared the
death, they have borne life away; and where they
would be safe, they perish. Then if they die
unprovided, no more is the King guilty of their damnation than he was before guilty of those impieties for
the which they are now visited. Every subject's duty is 170
the King's, but every subject's soul is his own. Therefore should every soldier in the wars do as every sick
man in his bed, wash every mote out of his conscience:
and dying so, death is to him advantage; or not dying,
the time was blessedly lost, wherein such preparation
was gained; and in him that escapes, it were not sin to
think that, making God so free an offer, He let him
outlive that day, to see His greatness, and to teach
others how they should prepare.

WILLIAMS   'Tis certain, every man that dies ill, the ill upon his own 180
           head, the King is not to answer it.

BATES   I do not desire he should answer for me, and yet I
           determine to fight lustily for him.

KING   I myself heard the King say he would not be ransomed.

WILLIAMS   Ay, he said so, to make us fight cheerfully; but when
           our throats are cut, he may be ransomed, and we ne'er
           the wiser.

KING   If I live to see it, I will never trust his word after.

WILLIAMS   You pay him then! That's a perilous shot out of an
           elder-gun,[127] that a poor and a private displeasure can 190
           do against a monarch! You may as well go about to turn
           the sun to ice, with fanning in his face with a peacock's
           feather. You'll never trust his word after! Come, 'tis a
           foolish saying.

KING   Your reproof is something too round: I should be
           angry with you, if the time were convenient.

WILLIAMS   Let it be a quarrel between us, if you live.

KING   I embrace it.

WILLIAMS How shall I know thee again?

KING Give me any gage of thine, and I will wear it in my   200
bonnet: then, if ever thou dar'st acknowledge it, I will
make it my quarrel.

WILLIAMS Here's my glove; give me another of thine.

KING There.

WILLIAMS This will I also wear in my cap. If ever thou come to
me and say, after tomorrow, 'This is my glove', by this
hand I will take thee a box on the ear.

KING If ever I live to see it, I will challenge it.

WILLIAMS Thou dar'st as well be hanged.

KING • Well, I will do it, though I take thee in the King's   210
company.

WILLIAMS Keep thy word; fare thee well.

BATES Be friends, you English fools, be friends; we have
French quarrels enow, if you could tell how to reckon.

KING Indeed, the French may lay twenty French crowns[128]
to one, they will beat us, for they bear them on their
shoulders; but it is no English treason to cut French
crowns,[129] and tomorrow the King himself will be a
clipper.   [Exeunt soldiers.

Upon the King! Let us our lives, our souls,   220
Our debts, our careful wives,
Our children, and our sins, lay on the King!
We must bear all. O hard condition,
Twin-born with greatness: subject to the breath
Of every fool, whose sense no more can feel
But his own wringing. What infinite heart's ease
Must kings neglect that private men enjoy?
And what have kings, that privates have not too,
Save ceremony, save general ceremony?[130]
And what art thou, thou idol Ceremony?   230
What kind of god art thou, that suffer'st more
Of mortal griefs than do thy worshippers?
What are thy rents? What are thy comings-in?
O Ceremony, show me but thy worth!
What is thy soul of adoration?
Art thou aught else but place, degree, and form,
Creating awe and fear in other men?

Wherein thou art less happy, being feared,
Than they in fearing.
What drink'st thou oft, instead of homage sweet,   240
But poisoned flattery? O, be sick, great greatness,
And bid thy ceremony give thee cure!
Thinkst thou the fiery fever will go out
With titles blown from adulation?
Will it give place to flexure and low bending?
Canst thou, when thou command'st the beggar's knee,
Command the health of it? No, thou proud dream,
That play'st so subtly with a king's repose.
I am a king that find thee; and I know,
'Tis not the balm, the sceptre, and the ball,   250
The sword, the mace, the crown imperial,
The intertissued robe of gold and pearl,
The farcèd title running 'fore the King,[131]
The throne he sits on, nor the tide of pomp
That beats upon the high shore of this world:
No, not all these, thrice-gorgeous ceremony,
Not all these, laid in bed majestical,
Can sleep so soundly as the wretched slave,
Who, with a body filled, and vacant mind,
Gets him to rest, crammed with distressful bread;   260
Never sees horrid night, the child of hell,
But, like a lackey, from the rise to set,
Sweats in the eye of Phoebus, and all night
Sleeps in Elysium; next day, after dawn,
Doth rise, and help Hyperion[132] to his horse;
And follows so the ever-running year
With profitable labour to his grave:
And, but for ceremony, such a wretch,
Winding up days with toil, and nights with sleep,
Had the fore-hand and vantage of a king.   270
The slave, a member of the country's peace,
Enjoys it; but in gross brain little wots
What watch the King keeps to maintain the peace,
Whose hours the peasant best advantages.[133]

Enter ERPINGHAM.

ERPING.   My lord, your nobles, jealous of your absence,
          Seek through your camp to find you.
KING   Good old knight,
          Collect them all together at my tent.
          I'll be before thee.
ERPING.   I shall do't, my lord.   [*Exit.*
KING   O God of battles, steel my soldiers' hearts;
          Possess them not with fear. Take from them now   280
          The sense of reck'ning, ere th'opposèd numbers
          Pluck their hearts from them. Not today, O Lord,
          O, not today, think not upon the fault
          My father made in compassing the crown.[134]
          I Richard's body have interrèd new,
          And on it have bestowed more contrite tears
          Than from it issued forcèd drops of blood.
          Five hundred poor I have in yearly pay,
          Who twice a day their withered hands hold up
          Toward heaven, to pardon blood; and I have built   290
          Two chantries, where the sad and solemn priests
          Sing still for Richard's soul. More will I do;
          Though all that I can do is nothing worth,
          Since that my penitence comes after all,
          Imploring pardon.

                    Enter GLOUCESTER.

GLO'STER   My liege!
KING   My brother Gloucester's voice? Ay:
          I know thy errand; I will go with thee.
          The day, my friends, and all things stay for me.
                                                    [*Exeunt.*

SCENE 2

The French camp.

Enter the DOLPHIN, ORLEANCE, RAMBURES, *and* BEAUMONT.

ORLEANCE	The sun doth gild our armour. Up, my lords!
DOLPHIN	Montez à cheval! My horse! Varlet! Laquais! Ha![135]
ORLEANCE	O brave spirit!
DOLPHIN	Via! Les eaux et terre![136]
ORLEANCE	Rien puis? L'air et feu?[137]
DOLPHIN	Cieux,[138] cousin Orleance!

Enter CONSTABLE.

Now, my Lord Constable?

CONSTABLE	Hark how our steeds for present service neigh!	
DOLPHIN	Mount them, and make incision in their hides,	
	That their hot blood may spin in English eyes,	10
	And dout them with superfluous courage. Ha!	
RAMBURES	What, will you have them weep our horses' blood?	
	How shall we then behold their natural tears?	

Enter MESSENGER.

MESSENGER	The English are embattled, you French peers.	
CONSTABLE	To horse, you gallant princes, straight to horse!	
	Do but behold yon poor and starvèd band,	
	And your fair show shall suck away their souls,	
	Leaving them but the shales and husks of men.	
	There is not work enough for all our hands,	
	Scarce blood enough in all their sickly veins	20
	To give each naked curtle-axe a stain,	
	That our French gallants shall today draw out	
	And sheathe for lack of sport. Let us but blow on them,	
	The vapour of our valour will o'erturn them.	
	'Tis positive 'gainst all exceptions, lords,	
	That our superfluous lackeys and our peasants,	
	Who in unnecessary action swarm	
	About our squares of battle, were enow	
	To purge this field of such a hilding foe,	
	Though we upon this mountain's basis by	30
	Took stand for idle speculation –	

But that our honours must not. What's to say?
A very little little let us do,
And all is done. Then let the trumpets sound
The tucket sonance and the note to mount:[139]
For our approach shall so much dare the field
That England shall couch down in fear, and yield.

Enter GRANDPRÉ.

GRANDPRÉ Why do you stay so long, my lords of France?
Yon island carrions, desperate of their bones,
Ill-favouredly become the morning field: 40
Their ragged curtains[140] poorly are let loose,
And our air shakes them passing scornfully.
Big Mars[141] seems bankrout in their beggared host,
And faintly through a rusty beaver peeps.
The horsemen sit like fixèd candlesticks
With torch-staves in their hand; and their poor jades
Lob down their heads, dropping the hides and hips,
The gum down-roping from their pale-dead eyes,
And in their pale dull mouths the gimmaled bit
Lies foul with chawed-grass, still and motionless;   50
And their executors, the knavish crows,
Fly o'er them all, impatient for their hour.
Description cannot suit itself in words
To demonstrate the life of such a battle,
In life so lifeless as it shows itself.

CONSTABLE They have said their prayers, and they stay for death.

DOLPHIN Shall we go send them dinners and fresh suits,
And give their fasting horses provender,
And after fight with them?

CONSTABLE I stay but for my guidon;[142] to the field!   60
I will the banner from a trumpet take,
And use it for my haste. Come, come away!
The sun is high, and we outwear the day.

                                        [*Exeunt.*

SCENE 3.

The English camp.

Enter GLOUCESTER, BEDFORD, EXETER, ERPINGHAM *with all his host;*
SALISBURY *and* WESTMORLAND, *with others.*

GLO'STER   Where is the King?
BEDFORD   The King himself is rode to view their battle.
WEST'LAND   Of fighting men they have full three-score thousand.
EXETER   There's five to one; besides, they all are fresh.
SALISBURY   God's arm strike with us! 'Tis a fearful odds.
　　　　　God buy you, princes all; I'll to my charge.
　　　　　If we no more meet till we meet in heaven,
　　　　　Then joyfully, my noble Lord of Bedford,
　　　　　My dear Lord Gloucester, and my good Lord Exeter,
　　　　　And my kind kinsman, warriors all, adieu!   10
BEDFORD   Farewell, good Salisbury, and good luck go with thee!
EXETER   Farewell, kind lord; fight valiantly today –
　　　　　And yet I do thee wrong, to mind thee of it,
　　　　　For thou art framed of the firm truth of valour.[143]
　　　　　　　　　　　　　　　　　　　　　[Exit Salisbury.
BEDFORD   He is as full of valour as of kindness;
　　　　　Princely in both.

　　　　　　　　　　　Enter the KING.

WEST'LAND   　　　　　　　　O that we now had here
　　　　　But one ten thousand of those men in England
　　　　　That do no work today!
KING   　　　　　　　　　　What's he that wishes so?
　　　　　My cousin Westmorland? No, my fair cousin:
　　　　　If we are marked to die, we are enow   20
　　　　　To do our country loss; and, if to live,
　　　　　The fewer men, the greater share of honour.
　　　　　God's will, I pray thee wish not one man more.
　　　　　By Jove, I am not covetous for gold,
　　　　　Nor care I who doth feed upon my cost:
　　　　　It ernes me not if men my garments wear;
　　　　　Such outward things dwell not in my desires.
　　　　　But if it be a sin to covet honour,

I am the most offending soul alive.
No, faith, my coz, wish not a man from England: 30
God's peace, I would not lose so great an honour
As one man more, methinks, would share from me,
For the best hope I have. O, do not wish one more.
Rather proclaim it, Westmorland, through my host,
That he which hath no stomach to this fight,
Let him depart; his passport shall be made,
And crowns for convoy put into his purse:
We would not die in that man's company
That fears his fellowship to die with us.[144]
This day is called the feast of Crispian:[145]   40
He that outlives this day, and comes safe home,
Will stand a-tiptoe when this day is named,
And rouse him at the name of Crispian.
He that shall see this day, and live old age,
Will yearly on the vigil feast his neighbours,
And say, 'Tomorrow is Saint Crispian.'
Then will he strip his sleeve, and show his scars,
And say, 'These wounds I had on Crispin's day.'
Old men forget; yet all shall be forgot,
But he'll remember, with advantages,   50
What feats he did that day. Then shall our names,
Familiar in his mouth as household words,
Harry the King, Bedford and Exeter,
Warwick and Talbot, Salisbury and Gloucester,
Be in their flowing cups freshly remembered.
This story shall the good man teach his son;
And Crispin Crispian[146] shall ne'er go by,
From this day to the ending of the world,
But we in it shall be rememberèd;
We few, we happy few, we band of brothers: 60
For he today that sheds his blood with me
Shall be my brother: be he ne'er so vile,
This day shall gentle his condition;
And gentlemen in England, now a-bed,
Shall think themselves accursed they were not here,
And hold their manhoods cheap whiles any speaks
That fought with us upon Saint Crispin's day.

Enter SALISBURY.

SALISBURY   My sovereign lord, bestow yourself with speed:
            The French are bravely in their battles set,
            And will with all expedience charge on us.   70
KING   All things are ready, if our minds be so.
WEST'LAND   Perish the man whose mind is backward now!
KING   Thou dost not wish more help from England, coz?
WEST'LAND   God's will, my liege, would you and I alone,
            Without more help, could fight this royal battle!
KING   Why, now thou hast unwished five thousand men;
            Which likes me better than to wish us one.
            You know your places: God be with you all!

Tucket. Enter MONTJOY.

MONTJOY   Once more I come to know of thee, King Harry,
            If for thy ransom thou wilt now compound,   80
            Before thy most assured overthrow:
            For certainly, thou art so near the gulf,
            Thou needs must be englutted. Besides, in mercy,
            The Constable desires thee thou wilt mind
            Thy followers of repentance; that their souls
            May make a peaceful and a sweet retire
            From off these fields, where (wretches) their poor bodies
            Must lie and fester.
KING   Who hath sent thee now?
MONTJOY   The Constable of France.
KING   I pray thee bear my former answer back: 90
            Bid them achieve me, and then sell my bones.
            Good God, why should they mock poor fellows thus?
            The man that once did sell the lion's skin
            While the beast lived, was killed with hunting him.
            A many of our bodies shall no doubt
            Find native graves: upon the which, I trust,
            Shall witness live in brass of this day's work.
            And those that leave their valiant bones in France,
            Dying like men, though buried in your dunghills,
            They shall be famed: for there the sun shall greet them,   100
            And draw their honours reeking up to heaven,
            Leaving their earthly parts to choke your clime,

The smell whereof shall breed a plague in France.
Mark then abounding valour in our English:
That being dead, like to the bullets crazing,[147]
Break out into a second course of mischief,
Killing in relapse of mortality.[148]
Let me speak proudly: tell the Constable
We are but warriors for the working-day:
Our gayness and our gilt are all besmirched   110
With rainy marching in the painful field.
There's not a piece of feather in our host –
Good argument (I hope) we will not fly –
And time hath worn us into slovenry.
But, by the Mass, our hearts are in the trim;
And my poor soldiers tell me, yet ere night
They'll be in fresher robes, or they will pluck
The gay new coats o'er the French soldiers' heads,
And turn them out of service. If they do this –
As, if God please, they shall – my ransom then   120
Will soon be levied. Herald, save thou thy labour:
Come thou no more for ransom, gentle herald;
They shall have none, I swear, but these my joints:
Which, if they have as I will leave 'em them,
Shall yield them little. Tell the Constable.

MONTJOY   I shall, King Harry. And so fare thee well;
Thou never shalt hear herald any more.   [Exit.

KING   I fear thou wilt once more come again for a ransom.

Enter YORK.

YORK   My lord, most humbly on my knee I beg   130
The leading of the vaward.

KING   Take it, brave York. Now soldiers, march away;
And how thou pleasest, God, dispose the day!
                                                    [Exeunt.

SCENE 4.

The field of battle.

Alarum. Excursions. Enter PISTOL, FRENCH SOLDIER, *and* BOY.

PISTOL	Yield, cur.
FR. SOLD.	Je pense que vous êtes le gentilhomme de bonne qualité.[149]
PISTOL	Qualtitie! Calen o custure me![150] Art thou a gentleman?
	What is thy name? Discuss.
FR. SOLD.	O Seigneur Dieu![151]
PISTOL	O, Signieur Dew should be a gentleman.
	Perpend my words, O Signieur Dew, and mark:
	O Signieur Dew, thou diest on point of fox,
	Except, O Signieur, thou do give to me
	Egregious ransom.
FR. SOLD.	O, prenez miséricorde! Ayez pitié de moi![152]
PISTOL	Moy[153] shall not serve; I will have forty moys,
	Or I will fetch thy rim[154] out at thy throat
	In drops of crimson blood.
FR. SOLD.	Est-il impossible d'échapper à la force de ton bras?[155]
PISTOL	Brass, cur?[156]
	Thou damnèd and luxurious mountain goat,
	Offer'st me brass?
FR. SOLD.	O pardonnez-moi![157]
PISTOL	Say'st thou me so? Is that a ton of moys?
	Come hither, boy, ask me this slave in French
	What is his name.
BOY	Écoutez: comment êtes-vous appelé?[158]
FR. SOLD.	Monsieur le Fer.
BOY	He says his name is Master Fer.
PISTOL	Master Fer! I'll fer him, and firk him, and ferret him![159]
	Discuss the same in French unto him.
BOY	I do not know the French for fer, and ferret, and firk.
PISTOL	Bid him prepare, for I will cut his throat.
FR. SOLD.	Que dit-il, monsieur?[160]
BOY	Il me commande à vous dire que vous faites vous prêt,
	car ce soldat ici est disposé tout à cette heure de couper
	votre gorge.[161]
PISTOL	Oui, couper la gorge, par ma foi,[162]

10

20

30

Peasant, unless thou give me crowns, brave crowns;
Or mangled shalt thou be by this my sword.

FR. SOLD. O, je vous supplie, pour l'amour de Dieu, me pardonner! Je suis le gentilhomme de bonne maison:
gardez ma vie, et je vous donnerai deux cents écus.[163]

PISTOL What are his words?   40

BOY He prays you to save his life; he is a gentleman of a
good house; and for his ransom he will give you two
hundred crowns.

PISTOL Tell him my fury shall abate, and I
The crowns will take.

FR. SOLD. Petit monsieur, que dit-il?[164]

BOY Encore qu'il est contre son jurement de pardonner
aucun prisonnier; néanmoins, pour les écus que vous
lui promettez, il est content à vous donner la liberté, le
franchisement.[165]   50

FR. SOLD. Sur mes genoux je vous donne mille remerciements, et
je m'estime heureux que je suis tombé entre les mains
d'un chevalier, je pense, le plus brave, vaillant, et très
distingué seigneur d'Angleterre.[166]

PISTOL Expound unto me, boy.

BOY He gives you upon his knees a thousand thanks, and he
esteems himself happy that he hath fallen into the
hands of one, as he thinks, the most brave, valorous,
and thrice-worthy signieur of England.

PISTOL As I suck blood, I will some mercy show. Follow me!   60

BOY Suivez-vous le grand capitaine![167]

[Exeunt Pistol and French soldier.
I did never know so full a voice issue from so empty a
heart; but the saying is true, 'The empty vessel makes
the greatest sound.' Bardolph and Nym had ten times
more valour than this roaring devil i'th'old play, that
every one may pare his nails with a wooden dagger,[168]
and they are both hanged, and so would this be, if he
durst steal any thing adventurously. I must stay with
the lackeys with the luggage of our camp. The French
might have a good prey of us, if he knew of it, for there 70
is none to guard it but boys.

[Exit.

SCENE 5.

Enter CONSTABLE, ORLEANCE, BOURBON,
DOLPHIN, *and* RAMBURES.

CONSTABLE   O diable!

ORLEANCE   O Seigneur! Le jour est perdu, tout est perdu!

DOLPHIN   Mort de ma vie!¹⁶⁹ All is confounded, all!
Reproach and everlasting shame
Sits mocking in our plumes.   [*A short alarum.*
O méchante fortune!¹⁷⁰ Do not run away.

CONSTABLE   Why, all our ranks are broke.

DOLPHIN   O perdurable shame! Let's stab ourselves.
Be these the wretches that we played at dice for?

ORLEANCE   Is this the King we sent to for his ransom?   10

BOURBON   Shame, and eternal shame, nothing but shame!
Let us die! In once more! Ay, back again,¹⁷¹
And he that will not follow Bourbon now,
Let him go hence, and, with his cap in hand,
Like a base pandar hold the chamber-door
Whilst, by a slave no gentler than my dog,
His fairest daughter is contaminated.

CONSTABLE   Disorder, that hath spoiled us, friend us now!
Let us on heaps go offer up our lives.

ORLEANCE   We are enow yet living in the field   20
To smother up the English in our throngs,
If any order might be thought upon.

BOURBON   The devil take order now! I'll to the throng.
Let life be short, else shame will be too long.

                          [*Exeunt.*

SCENE 6.

Alarum. Enter the KING *and his train, with prisoners;*
*   EXETER and others.*

KING   Well have we done, thrice-valiant countrymen,
              But all's not done – yet keep the French the field.

EXETER   The Duke of York commends him to your Majesty.

KING   Lives he, good uncle? Thrice within this hour
              I saw him down; thrice up again, and fighting;
              From helmet to the spur all blood he was.

EXETER   In which array (brave soldier) doth he lie,
              Larding the plain: and by his bloody side
              (Yoke-fellow to his honour-owing wounds)
              The noble Earl of Suffolk also lies.   10
              Suffolk first died, and York, all haggled over,
              Comes to him, where in gore he lay insteeped,
              And takes him by the beard, kisses the gashes
              That bloodily did yawn upon his face,
              And cries aloud, 'Tarry, my cousin Suffolk!
              My soul shall thine keep company to heaven;
              Tarry, sweet soul, for mine, then fly abreast,
              As in this glorious and well-foughten field
              We kept together in our chivalry.'
              Upon these words I came, and cheered him up;   20
              He smiled me in the face, raught me his hand,
              And, with a feeble grip, says, 'Dear my lord,
              Commend my service to my sovereign.'
              So did he turn, and over Suffolk's neck
              He threw his wounded arm, and kissed his lips;
              And so, espoused to death, with blood he sealed
              A testament of noble-ending love.
              The pretty and sweet manner of it forced
              Those waters from me which I would have stopped,
              But I had not so much of man in me,   30
              And all my mother came into mine eyes [172]
              And gave me up to tears.

KING   I blame you not,
              For, hearing this, I must perforce compound

With mistful eyes,[173] or they will issue too.   [*Alarum.*
But hark, what new alarum is this same?
The French have reinforced their scattered men.
Then every soldier kill his prisoners:[174]
Give the word through.

                                                                        [*Exeunt.*

SCENE 7.

Enter FLUELLEN *and* GOWER.

FLUELLEN   Kill the poys and the luggage![175] 'Tis expressly against the
law of arms: 'tis as arrant a piece of knavery, mark you
now, as can be offert. In your conscience now, is it not?

GOWER   'Tis certain, there's not a boy left alive, and the cowardly rascals that ran from the battle ha' done this
slaughter; besides, they have burned and carried away
all that was in the King's tent: wherefore the King,
most worthily, hath caused every soldier to cut his
prisoner's throat. O, 'tis a gallant king!

FLUELLEN   Ay, he was porn at Monmouth, Captain Gower. What call   10
you the town's name where Alexander the Pig was born?

GOWER   Alexander the Great.

FLUELLEN   Why, I pray you, is not 'pig' great? The pig, or the great,
or the mighty, or the huge, or the magnanimous, are all
one reckonings, save the phrase is a little variations.

GOWER   I think Alexander the Great was born in Macedon; his
father was called Philip of Macedon, as I take it.

FLUELLEN   I think it is in Macedon where Alexander is porn. I tell
you, captain, if you look in the maps of the 'orld, I
warrant you sall find, in the comparisons between   20
Macedon and Monmouth, that the situations, look you,
is both alike. There is a river in Macedon, and there is
also moreover a river at Monmouth. It is called Wye at
Monmouth; but it is out of my prains what is the name
of the other river; but 'tis all one, 'tis alike as my fingers
is to my fingers, and there is salmons in both. If you
mark Alexander's life well, Harry of Monmouth's life is
come after it indifferent well, for there is figures in all

things. Alexander, God knows, and you know, in his
rages, and his furies, and his wraths, and his cholers, and   30
his moods, and his displeasures, and his indignations,
and also being a little intoxicates in his prains, did in his
ales and his angers (look you) kill his best friend Cleitus.

GOWER   Our King is not like him in that; he never killed any of
           his friends.

FLUELLEN   It is not well done (mark you now) to take the tales out
           of my mouth, ere it is made and finished. I speak but in
           the figures and comparisons of it: as Alexander killed
           his friend Cleitus,[176] being in his ales and his cups, so
           also Harry Monmouth, being in his right wits and his   40
           good judgements, turned away the fat knight with the
           great-belly doublet: he was full of jests, and gipes, and
           knaveries, and mocks; I have forgot his name.

GOWER   Sir John Falstaff.

FLUELLEN   That is he. I'll tell you, there is good men porn at
           Monmouth.

GOWER   Here comes his Majesty.

Alarum. Enter KING HARRY *with* BOURBON *and other prisoners;*
WARWICK, GLOUCESTER, EXETER, *heralds and soldiers. Flourish.*

KING   I was not angry since I came to France,
           Until this instant. Take a trumpet, herald;
           Ride thou unto the horsemen on yon hill: 50
           If they will fight with us, bid them come down
           Or void the field: they do offend our sight.
           If they'll do neither, we will come to them,
           And make them skirr away as swift as stones
           Enforcèd from the old Assyrian slings.[177]
           Besides, we'll cut the throats of those we have,
           And not a man of them that we shall take
           Shall taste our mercy. Go and tell them so.

                                              [*Exit a herald.*

                          Enter MONTJOY.

EXETER   Here comes the herald of the French, my liege.

GLO'STER   His eyes are humbler than they used to be.   60

KING   How now, what means this, herald? Know'st thou not

That I have fined these bones of mine for ransom?
Com'st thou again for ransom?

MONTJOY   No, great King:
I come to thee for charitable licence,
That we may wander o'er this bloody field,
To book our dead, and then to bury them;
To sort our nobles from our common men;
For many of our princes (woe the while!)
Lie drowned and soaked in mercenary blood:
So do our vulgar drench their peasant limbs   70
In blood of princes, and their wounded steeds
Fret fetlock deep in gore, and with wild rage
Yerk out their armèd heels at their dead masters,
Killing them twice. O, give us leave, great King,
To view the field in safety, and dispose
Of their dead bodies.

KING   I tell thee truly, herald,
I know not if the day be ours or no,
For yet a many of your horsemen peer
And gallop o'er the field.

MONTJOY   The day is yours.

KING   Praisèd be God, and not our strength, for it!   80
What is this castle called that stands hard by?

MONTJOY   They call it Agincourt.

KING   Then call we this the field of Agincourt,
Fought on the day of Crispin Crispianus.

FLUELLEN   Your grandfather[178] of famous memory (an't please
your Majesty) and your great-uncle Edward the Plack
Prince of Wales, as I have read in the chronicles,
fought a most prave pattle here in France.

KING   They did, Fluellen.

FLUELLEN   Your Majesty says very true. If your Majesties is re- 90
membered of it, the Welshmen did good service in a
garden where leeks did grow, wearing leeks in their
Monmouth caps, which, your Majesty know, to this
hour is an honourable badge of the service; and I do
believe your majesty takes no scorn to wear the leek
upon Saint Tavy's day.

KING   I wear it for a memorable honour:

For I am Welsh, you know, good countryman.

FLUELLEN   All the water in Wye cannot wash your Majesty's
Welsh plood out of your pody, I can tell you that. God   100
pless it, and preserve it, as long as it pleases His grace,
and His majesty too![179]

KING   Thanks, good my countryman.

FLUELLEN   By Jeshu, I am your Majesty's countryman; I care not
who know it: I will confess it to all the 'orld. I need not
to be ashamed of your Majesty, praised be God, so
long as your Majesty is an honest man.

KING   God keep me so.

Enter WILLIAMS.

Our heralds go with him:
Bring me just notice of the numbers dead
On both our parts.   [*Exeunt heralds with Montjoy.*
Call yonder fellow hither.   110

EXETER   Soldier, you must come to the King.

KING   Soldier, why wear'st thou that glove in thy cap?

WILLIAMS   An't please your Majesty, 'tis the gage of one that I
should fight withal, if he be alive.

KING   An Englishman?

WILLIAMS   An't please your Majesty, a rascal that swaggered with
me last night: who, if a live and ever dare to challenge
this glove, I have sworn to take him a box o'th'ear; or
if I can see my glove in his cap – which he swore, as he
was a soldier, he would wear if alive – I will strike it   120
out soundly.

KING   What think you, Captain Fluellen? Is it fit this soldier
keep his oath?

FLUELLEN   He is a craven and a villain else, an't please your
Majesty, in my conscience.

KING   It may be his enemy is a gentleman of great sort, quite
from the answer of his degree.[180]

FLUELLEN   Though he be as good a gentleman as the devil is,[181] as
Lucifer and Belzebub[182] himself, it is necessary, look
your Grace, that he keep his vow and his oath. If he be   130
perjured (see you now), his reputation is as arrant a
villain and a Jack-sauce as ever his black shoe trod upon

God's ground and His earth, in my conscience, law!

KING   Then keep thy vow, sirrah, when thou meet'st the fellow.

WILLIAMS   So I will, my liege, as I live.

KING   Who serv'st thou under?

WILLIAMS   Under Captain Gower, my liege.

FLUELLEN   Gower is a good captain, and is good knowledge and
            literatured in the wars.

KING   Call him hither to me, soldier.   140

WILLIAMS   I will, my liege.   [*Exit.*

KING   Here, Fluellen, wear thou this favour for me, and stick
            it in thy cap. When Alanson and myself were down
            together, I plucked this glove from his helm. If any
            man challenge this, he is a friend to Alanson, and an
            enemy to our person; if thou encounter any such,
            apprehend him, an thou dost me love.

FLUELLEN   Your Grace does me as great honours as can be desired
            in the hearts of his subjects. I would fain see the man
            that has but two legs that shall find himself aggriefed at   150
            this glove, that is all; but I would fain see it once, an't
            please God of His grace that I might see.

KING   Know'st thou Gower?

FLUELLEN   He is my dear friend, an't please you.

KING   Pray thee, go seek him, and bring him to my tent.

FLUELLEN   I will fetch him.   [*Exit.*

KING   My Lord of Warwick, and my brother Gloucester,
            Follow Fluellen closely at the heels.
            The glove which I have given him for a favour
            May haply purchase him a box o'th'ear.   160
            It is the soldier's; I by bargain should
            Wear it myself. Follow, good cousin Warwick:
            If that the soldier strike him, as I judge
            By his blunt bearing he will keep his word,
            Some sudden mischief may arise of it;
            For I do know Fluellen valiant,
            And, touched with choler, hot as gunpowder,
            And quickly will return an injury.
            Follow, and see there be no harm between them.
            Go you with me, uncle of Exeter.   170

                                                       [*Exeunt.*

SCENE 8.

Enter GOWER *and* WILLIAMS.

WILLIAMS   I warrant it is to knight you, captain.

Enter FLUELLEN.

FLUELLEN   God's will, and His pleasure, captain, I beseech you
now, come apace to the King: there is more good
toward you, peradventure, than is in your knowledge
to dream of.

WILLIAMS   [*points to his own cap.*] Sir, know you this glove?

FLUELLEN   Know the glove? I know the glove is a glove.

WILLIAMS   [*points to Fluellen's cap.*]
I know this, and thus I challenge it.   [*Strikes him.*

FLUELLEN   'Sblood, an arrant traitor as any's in the universal
world, or in France, or in England!   10

GOWER   How now, sir? You villain!

WILLIAMS   Do you think I'll be forsworn?

FLUELLEN   Stand away, Captain Gower, I will give treason his
payment into plows, I warrant you.

WILLIAMS   I am no traitor.

FLUELLEN   That's a lie in thy throat. I charge you in his Majesty's
name, apprehend him: he's a friend of the Duke
Alanson's.

Enter WARWICK *and* GLOUCESTER, *with the* KING
and EXETER *following.*

WARWICK   How now, how now, what's the matter?

FLUELLEN   My Lord of Warwick, here is, praised be God for it, a   20
most contagious treason come to light, look you, as you
shall desire in a summer's day. Here is his Majesty.

KING   Now now, what's the matter?

FLUELLEN   My liege, here is a villain and a traitor, that, look your
Grace, has struck the glove which your majesty is take
out of the helmet of Alanson.

WILLIAMS   My liege, this was my glove; here is the fellow of it;
and he that I gave it to in change promised to wear it in
his cap. I promised to strike him, if he did. I met this

	man with my glove in his cap, and I have been as good 30
	as my word.
FLUELLEN	Your Majesty, hear now, saving your Majesty's man-
	hood, what an arrant, rascally, beggarly, lousy knave it is.
	I hope your Majesty is pear me testimony and witness,
	and will avouchment, that this is the glove of Alanson
	that your Majesty is give me, in your conscience now.
KING	Give me thy glove, soldier. Look, here is the fellow of it.
	'Twas I indeed thou promised'st to strike,
	And thou hast given me most bitter terms.
FLUELLEN	An't please your Majesty, let his neck answer for it, if 40
	there is any martial law in the world.
KING	How canst thou make me satisfaction?
WILLIAMS	All offences, my lord, come from the heart. Never
	came any from mine that might offend your Majesty.
KING	It was ourself thou didst abuse.
WILLIAMS	Your Majesty came not like yourself: you appeared to
	me but as a common man: witness the night, your
	garments, your lowliness; and what your Highness
	suffered under that shape, I beseech you take it for
	your own fault, and not mine: for had you been as I 50
	took you for, I made no offence; therefore I beseech
	your Highness pardon me.
KING	Here, uncle Exeter, fill this glove with crowns,
	And give it to this fellow. Keep it, fellow,
	And wear it for an honour in thy cap,
	Till I do challenge it. Give him the crowns;
	And, captain, you must needs be friends with him.
FLUELLEN	By this day and this light, the fellow has mettle enough in
	his belly. Hold, there is twelve-pence for you, and I pray
	you to serve God, and keep you out of prawls and 60
	prabbles, and quarrels and dissensions, and I warrant you
	it is the better for you.
WILLIAMS	I will none of your money.
FLUELLEN	It is with a good will; I can tell you it will serve you to
	mend your shoes. Come, wherefore should you be so
	pashful? Your shoes is not so good. 'Tis a good silling,
	I warrant you, or I will change it.

Enter an English Herald.

KING   Now, herald, are the dead numbered?
HERALD   Here is the number of the slaughtered French.
                              [*He delivers a paper.*
KING   What prisoners of good sort are taken, uncle?   70
EXETER   Charles Duke of Orleance, nephew to the king,
          John Duke of Bourbon, and Lord Bouciqualt;
          Of other lords and barons, knights and squires,
          Full fifteen hundred, besides common men.
KING   This note doth tell me of ten thousand French
          That in the field lie slain. Of princes, in this number,
          And nobles bearing banners, there lie dead
          One hundred twenty-six; added to these,
          Of knights, esquires, and gallant gentlemen,
          Eight thousand and four hundred, of the which,   80
          Five hundred were but yesterday dubbed knights.
          So that, in these ten thousand they have lost,
          There are but sixteen hundred mercenaries;
          The rest are princes, barons, lords, knights, squires,
          And gentlemen of blood and quality.
          The names of those their nobles that lie dead:
          Charles Delabreth, High Constable of France,
          Jaques of Chatillion, Admiral of France,
          The master of the cross-bows, Lord Rambures,
          Great Master of France, the brave Sir Guichard Dolphin, 90
          John Duke of Alanson, Anthony Duke of Brabant,
          The brother to the Duke of Burgundy,
          And Edward Duke of Bar; of lusty earls,
          Grandpré and Roussi, Faulconbridge and Foix,
          Beaumont and Marle, Vaudemont and Lestrale.
          Here was a royal fellowship of death.
          Where is the number of our English dead?
                              [*The herald presents another paper.*
          Edward the Duke of York, the Earl of Suffolk,
          Sir Richard Ketly, Davy Gam, esquire;
          None else of name; and, of all other men,   100
          But five and twenty. O God, thy arm was here:
          And not to us, but to thy arm alone,
          Ascribe we all. When, without stratagem,

But in plain shock and even play of battle,
Was ever known so great and little loss,
On one part and on th'other? Take it, God,
For it is none but thine.

EXETER   'Tis wonderful.

KING   Come, go we in procession to the village;
              And be it death proclaimèd through our host
              To boast of this or take that praise from God   110
              Which is his only.

FLUELLEN   Is it not lawful, an't please your majesty, to tell how
              many is killed?

KING   Yes, captain; but with this acknowledgement,
              That God fought for us.

FLUELLEN   Yes: in my conscience, he did us great good.

KING   Do we all holy rites:
              Let there be sung 'Non nobis' and 'Te Deum';[183]
              The dead with charity enclosed in clay;
              And then to Callice, and to England then,   120
              Where ne'er from France arrived more happy men.

                                                              [*Exeunt.*

ACT 5. PROLOGUE.

Enter CHORUS.

CHORUS   Vouchsafe to those that have not read the story,
            That I may prompt them; and of such as have,
            I humbly pray them to admit th'excuse
            Of time, of numbers, and due course of things,
            Which cannot in their huge and proper life
            Be here presented. Now we bear the King
            Toward Callice: grant him there; there seen,
            Heave him away upon your wingèd thoughts,
            Athwart the sea. Behold, the English beach
            Pales in the flood with men, with wives and boys,   10
            Whose shouts and claps out-voice the
                                        deep-mouthed sea,
            Which, like a mighty whiffler 'fore the King,
            Seems to prepare his way: so let him land,
            And solemnly see him set on to London.
            So swift a pace hath thought, that even now
            You may imagine him upon Blackheath;[184]
            Where that his lords desire him to have borne
            His bruisèd helmet and his bended sword
            Before him through the city: he forbids it,
            Being free from vainness and self-glorious pride;   20
            Giving full trophy, signal, and ostent,
            Quite from himself, to God. But now behold,
            In the quick forge and working-house of thought,[185]
            How London doth pour out her citizens:
            The Mayor and all his brethren in best sort,
            Like to the senators of th'antique Rome
            With the plebeians swarming at their heels,
            Go forth and fetch their conqu'ring Caesar in:
            As, by a lower but loving likelihood,
            Were now the General of our gracious Empress[186] –   30
            As in good time he may – from Ireland coming,
            Bringing rebellion broachèd on his sword,
            How many would the peaceful city quit

To welcome him! Much more, and much more cause,
Did they this Harry. Now in London place him:
As yet the lamentation of the French
Invites the King of England's stay at home,
The Emperor's coming[187] in behalf of France
To order peace between them;[188] and omit
All the occurrences, whatever chanced,   40
Till Harry's back-return again to France.
There must we bring him; and myself have played
The interim, by rememb'ring you 'tis past.
Then brook abridgement, and your eyes advance,
After your thoughts, straight back again to France.

                             [*Exit.*

ACT 5, SCENE I.

France. The English camp.

Enter FLUELLEN *and* GOWER.

GOWER   Nay, that's right. But why wear you your leek today?
Saint Davy's day is past.

FLUELLEN   There is occasions and causes why and wherefore in all
things. I will tell you ass my friend, Captain Gower.
The rascally, scauld, beggarly, lousy, pragging knave
Pistol, which you and yourself, and all the world, know
to be no petter than a fellow, look you now, of no
merits: he is come to me, and prings me pread and salt
yesterday, look you, and bid me eat my leek. It was in a
place where I could not breed no contention with him; 10
but I will be so bold as to wear it in my cap till I see him
once again, and then I will tell him a little piece of my
desires.

Enter PISTOL.

GOWER   Why here he comes, swelling like a turkey-cock.

FLUELLEN   'Tis no matter for his swellings, nor his turkey-cocks.
God pless you, Ancient Pistol: you scurvy lousy knave,
God pless you.

PISTOL   Ha! Art thou bedlam? Dost thou thirst, base Troyan,

To have me fold up Parca's fatal web?[189]
Hence! I am qualmish at the smell of leek.   20

FLUELLEN   I peseech you heartily, scurvy lousy knave, at my desires,
and my requests, and my petitions, to eat, look you, this
leek. Because, look you, you do not love it, nor your
affections, and your appetites, and your digestions does
not agree with it, I would desire you to eat it.

PISTOL   Not for Cadwallader and all his goats.[190]

FLUELLEN   There is one goat for you. [Strikes him with a cudgel.]
Will you be so good, scauld knave, as eat it?

PISTOL   Base Troyan, thou shalt die.

FLUELLEN   You say very true, scauld knave, when God's will is. I   30
will desire you to live in the mean time, and eat your
victuals: come, there is sauce for it. [He strikes him again.]
You called me yesterday mountain-squire, but I will
make you today a squire of low degree. [He knocks him
down.] I pray you, fall to: if you can mock a leek, you
can eat a leek.

GOWER   Enough, captain, you have astonished him.

FLUELLEN   I say, I will make him eat some part of my leek, or I
will peat his pate four days. Bite, I pray you: it is good
for your green wound, and your ploody coxcomb.   40
                         [He thrusts the leek at his mouth.

PISTOL   Must I bite?

FLUELLEN   Yes, certainly, and out of doubt, and out of question
too, and ambiguities.

PISTOL   By this leek, I will most horribly revenge – [Fluellen
threatens him.] I eat and eat, I swear.

FLUELLEN   Eat, I pray you. Will you have some more sauce to
your leek? There is not enough leek to swear by.
                                        [He beats him again.

PISTOL   Quiet thy cudgel, thou dost see I eat.

FLUELLEN   Much good do you, scauld knave, heartily. Nay, pray
you throw none away: the skin is good for your broken   50
coxcomb. When you take occasions to see leeks hereafter, I pray you mock at 'em, that is all.

PISTOL   Good.

FLUELLEN   Ay, leeks is good. Hold you, there is a groat to heal
your pate.

PISTOL   Me, a groat?
FLUELLEN   Yes verily, and in truth you shall take it, or I have
            another leek in my pocket which you shall eat.
PISTOL   I take thy groat in earnest of revenge.[191]
FLUELLEN   If I owe you anything, I will pay you in cudgels: you 60
            shall be a woodmonger, and buy nothing of me but
            cudgels. God buy you, and keep you, and heal your
            pate.   [Exit.
PISTOL   All hell shall stir for this.
GOWER   Go, go, you are a counterfeit cowardly knave. Will
            you mock at an ancient tradition, begun upon an
            honourable respect and worn as a memorable trophy
            of predeceased valour, and dare not avouch in your
            deeds any of your words? I have seen you gleeking
            and galling at this gentleman[192] twice or thrice. You 70
            thought, because he could not speak English in the
            native garb, he could not therefore handle an English
            cudgel. You find it otherwise; and henceforth let a
            Welsh correction teach you a good English condition.
            Fare ye well.   [Exit.
PISTOL   Doth Fortune play the huswife with me now?[193]
            News have I that my Doll is dead[194]
            I'th'spital of a malady of France,[195]
            And there my rendezvous is quite cut off.
            Old I do wax, and from my weary limbs   80
            Honour is cudgelled. Well, bawd will I turn,
            And something lean to cutpurse of quick hand.
            To England will I steal, and there I'll steal:
            And patches will I get unto these scars,
            And swear I got them in the Gallia wars.   [Exit.

SCENE 2.

France. A royal palace.

Enter, at one door, KING HENRY, EXETER, BEDFORD, WARWICK,
and other Lords; at another, QUEEN ISABEL, *the* FRENCH KING, *the*
Princess KATHERINE, ALICE, *the* DUKE OF BURGUNDY, *and other French.*

KING   Peace to this meeting, wherefore we are met!
            Unto our brother France, and to our sister,
            Health and fair time of day; joy and good wishes
            To our most fair and princely cousin Katherine;
            And, as a branch and member of this royalty,
            By whom this great assembly is contrived,
            We do salute you, Duke of Burgundy;
            And, princes French, and peers, health to you all!

FR. KING Right joyous are we to behold your face,
            Most worthy brother England; fairly met;   10
            So are you, princes English, every one.

ISABEL   So happy be the issue, brother England,[196]
            Of this good day and of this gracious meeting,
            As we are now glad to behold your eyes:
            Your eyes which hitherto have borne in them
            Against the French, that met them in their bent,
            The fatal balls of murdering basilisks.[197]
            The venom of such looks, we fairly hope,
            Have lost their quality, and that this day
            Shall change all griefs and quarrels into love.   20

KING   To cry 'Amen' to that, thus we appear.

ISABEL   You English princes all, I do salute you.

BURGUNDY My duty to you both, on equal love.
            Great Kings of France and England: that I have laboured
            With all my wits, my pains, and strong endeavours,
            To bring your most imperial Majesties
            Unto this bar and royal interview,
            Your mightiness on both parts best can witness.
            Since then my office hath so far prevailed,
            That face to face, and royal eye to eye,   30
            You have congreeted. Let it not disgrace me,

If I demand, before this royal view,
What rub or what impediment there is,
Why that the naked, poor, and mangled Peace,
Dear nurse of arts, plenties, and joyful births,
Should not in this best garden of the world,
Our fertile France, put up her lovely visage?
Alas, she hath from France too long been chased,
And all her husbandry doth lie on heaps,[198]
Corrupting in its own fertility.   40
Her vine, the merry cheerer of the heart,
Unprunèd, dies; her hedges even-pleached,
Like prisoners wildly overgrown with hair,
Put forth disordered twigs: her fallow leas
The darnel, hemlock, and rank fumitory
Doth root upon, while that the coulter rusts,
That should deracinate such savagery;
The even mead, that erst brought sweetly forth
The freckled cowslip, burnet, and green clover,
Wanting the scythe, all uncorrected, rank,   50
Conceives by idleness, and nothing teems
But hateful docks, rough thistles, kecksies, burs,
Losing both beauty and utility.
And as our vineyards, fallows, meads, and hedges,
Defective in their natures, grow to wildness,
Even so our houses, and ourselves, and children,
Have lost, or do not learn, for want of time,
The sciences that should become our country,
But grow (like savages, as soldiers will,
That nothing do but meditate on blood)   60
To swearing and stern looks, diffused attire,
And everything that seems unnatural.
Which to reduce into our former favour,
You are assembled; and my speech entreats,
That I may know the let, why gentle Peace
Should not expel these inconveniences
And bless us with her former qualities.

KING   If, Duke of Burgundy, you would the peace,
Whose want gives growth to th'imperfections
Which you have cited, you must buy that peace   70

<table>
<tr><td></td><td>With full accord to all our just demands,
Whose tenours and particular effects
You have, enscheduled briefly, in your hands.</td><td></td></tr>
<tr><td>BURGUNDY</td><td>The King hath heard them: to the which, as yet,
There is no answer made.</td><td></td></tr>
<tr><td>KING</td><td>   Well then: the peace,
Which you before so urged, lies in his answer.</td><td></td></tr>
<tr><td>FR. KING</td><td>I have but with a cursitory eye
O'erglanced the articles. Pleaseth your Grace
To appoint some of your Council presently
To sit with us once more, with better heed
To resurvey them, we will suddenly
Pass our accept and peremptory answer.¹⁹⁹</td><td>80</td></tr>
<tr><td>KING</td><td>Brother, we shall. Go, uncle Exeter,
And brother Clarence, and you, brother Gloucester,
Warwick, and Huntingdon, go with the King,
And take with you free power, to ratify,
Augment, or alter, as your wisdoms best
Shall see advantageable for our dignity,
Anything in or out of our demands,
And we'll consign thereto. Will you, fair sister,
Go with the princes, or stay here with us?</td><td>90</td></tr>
<tr><td>ISABEL</td><td>Our gracious brother, I will go with them:
Haply a woman's voice may do some good,
When articles too nicely urged be stood on.</td><td></td></tr>
<tr><td>KING</td><td>Yet leave our cousin Katherine here with us.
She is our capital demand, comprised
Within the fore-rank of our articles.</td><td></td></tr>
<tr><td>ISABEL</td><td>She hath good leave.   [Exeunt all but King Henry,
                                                    Katherine, and Alice.</td><td></td></tr>
<tr><td>KING</td><td>   Fair Katherine, and most fair,
Will you vouchsafe to teach a soldier terms
Such as will enter at a lady's ear
And plead his love-suit to her gentle heart?</td><td>100</td></tr>
<tr><td>KATHERINE</td><td>Your Majesty shall mock at me: I cannot speak your
England.</td><td></td></tr>
<tr><td>KING</td><td>O fair Katherine, if you will love me soundly with
your French heart, I will be glad to hear you confess it</td><td></td></tr>
</table>

brokenly with your English tongue. Do you like me, Kate?

KATHERINE Pardonnez-moi,[200] I cannot tell vat is 'like me'.

KING An angel is like you, Kate, and you are like an angel.

KATHERINE Que dit-il? Que je suis semblable aux anges?   110

ALICE Oui, vraiment (sauf votre grâce), ainsi dit-il.[201]

KING I said so, dear Katherine, and I must not blush to affirm it.

KATHERINE O bon Dieu! Les langues des hommes sont pleines de tromperies.[202]

KING What says she, fair one? That the tongues of men are full of deceits?

ALICE Oui, dat de tongues of de mans is be full of deceits: dat is de Princess.

KING The Princess is the better Englishwoman.[203] I'faith, 120 Kate, my wooing is fit for thy understanding. I am glad thou canst speak no better English, for, if thou couldst, thou wouldst find me such a plain king that thou wouldst think I had sold my farm to buy my crown. I know no ways to mince it in love, but directly to say 'I love you'; then, if you urge me farther than to say 'Do you in faith?', I wear out my suit. Give me your answer, i'faith do, and so clap hands, and a bargain. How say you, lady?

KATHERINE Sauf votre honneur,[204] me understand vell.   130

KING Marry, if you would put me to verses, or to dance for your sake, Kate, why, you undid me. For the one, I have neither words nor measure; and for the other, I have no strength in measure, yet a reasonable measure in strength.[205] If I could win a lady at leap-frog, or by vaulting into my saddle with my armour on my back, under the correction of bragging be it spoken,[206] I should quickly leap into[207] a wife; or if I might buffet for my love, or bound my horse for her favours, I could lay on like a butcher, and sit like a jack-an-apes, 140 never off. But before God, Kate, I cannot look greenly, nor gasp out my eloquence, nor I have no cunning in protestation; only downright oaths, which I never use till urged, nor never break for urging. If

thou canst love a fellow of this temper, Kate, whose
face is not worth sun-burning, that never looks in his
glass for love of anything he sees there, let thine eye be
thy cook.[208] I speak to thee plain soldier: if thou canst
love me for this, take me; if not, to say to thee that I 150
shall die, is true; but, for thy love, by the Lord, no; yet
I love thee too. And while thou liv'st, dear Kate, take a
fellow of plain and uncoined constancy, for he perforce must do thee right, because he hath not the gift
to woo in other places: for these fellows of infinite
tongue, that can rhyme themselves into ladies' favours,
they do always reason themselves out again. What? A
speaker is but a prater, a rhyme is but a ballad; a good
leg will fall, a straight back will stoop, a black beard
will turn white, a curled pate will grow bald, a fair face 160
will wither, a full eye will wax hollow; but a good
heart, Kate, is the sun and the moon, or rather the sun
and not the moon: for it shines bright, and never
changes, but keeps his course truly. If thou would have
such a one, take me! And take me, take a soldier: take a
soldier, take a king. And what say'st thou then to my
love? Speak, my fair, and fairly, I pray thee.

KATHERINE Is it possible dat I sould love de enemy of France?

KING   No, it is not possible you should love the enemy of
France, Kate; but, in loving me, you should love the 170
friend of France: for I love France so well that I will
not part with a village of it; I will have it all mine: and,
Kate, when France is mine, and I am yours, then yours
is France, and you are mine.

KATHERINE I cannot tell wat is dat.

KING   No, Kate? I will tell thee in French, which I am sure
will hang upon my tongue like a new-married wife
about her husband's neck, hardly to be shook off. Je
quand j'ai le possession de France, et quand vous avez le
possession de moi[209] – let me see, what then? Saint 180
Dennis be my speed![210] – donc vôtre est France, et vous
êtes mienne.[211] It is as easy for me, Kate, to conquer the
kingdom, as to speak so much more French: I shall
never move thee in French, unless it be to laugh at me.

KATHERINE Sauf votre honneur, le français que vous parlez, il est meilleur que l'anglais lequel je parle.[212]

KING No, faith, is't not, Kate: but thy speaking of my tongue, and I thine, most truly falsely, must needs be granted to be much at one. But, Kate, dost thou understand thus much English? Canst thou love me?   190

KATHERINE I cannot tell.

KING Can any of your neighbours tell, Kate? I'll ask them. Come, I know thou lovest me: and at night, when you come into your closet, you'll question this gentle-woman about me; and I know, Kate, you will to her dispraise those parts in me that you love with your heart: but, good Kate, mock me mercifully, the rather, gentle Princess, because I love thee cruelly. If ever thou beest mine, Kate, as I have a saving faith within me tells me thou shalt, I get thee with scambling,[213] and thou   200 must therefore needs prove a good soldier-breeder. Shall not thou and I, between Saint Dennis and Saint George, compound a boy, half French, half English, that shall go to Constantinople, and take the Turk by the beard?[214] Shall we not? What say'st thou, my fair flower-de-luce?[215]

KATHERINE I do not know dat.

KING No; 'tis hereafter to know, but now to promise. Do but now promise, Kate, you will endeavour for your French part of such a boy; and, for my English moiety,   210 take the word of a king and a bachelor. How answer you, la plus belle Katherine du monde, mon très cher et devin déesse?[216]

KATHERINE Your majestee 'ave fausse[217] French enough to deceive de most sage demoiselle[218] dat is en France.

KING Now fie upon my false French! By mine honour, in true English, I love thee, Kate; by which honour, I dare not swear thou lovest me, yet my blood begins to flatter me that thou dost, notwithstanding the poor and untempering effect of my visage. Now beshrew my   220 father's ambition! He was thinking of civil wars when he got me, therefore was I created with a stubborn outside, with an aspect of iron, that when I come to

woo ladies, I fright them; but in faith, Kate, the elder I
wax, the better I shall appear. My comfort is, that old
age, that ill layer up of beauty, can do no more spoil
upon my face. Thou hast me, if thou hast me, at the
worst; and thou shalt wear me, if thou wear me, better
and better: and therefore tell me, most fair Katherine,
will you have me? Put off your maiden blushes,   230
avouch the thoughts of your heart with the looks of
an empress, take me by the hand, and say 'Harry of
England, I am thine': which word thou shalt no
sooner bless mine ear withal, but I will tell thee aloud,
'England is thine, Ireland is thine, France is thine, and
Henry Plantagenet[219] is thine'; who, though I speak it
before his face, if he be not fellow with the best king,
thou shalt find the best king of good fellows. Come,
your answer in broken music: for thy voice is music,
and thy English broken: therefore, queen of all,   240
Katherine, break thy mind to me in broken English:
wilt thou have me?

KATHERINE Dat is as it sall please de roi mon père.[220]

KING Nay, it will please him well, Kate; it shall please him,
Kate.

KATHERINE Den it sall also content me.

KING Upon that I kiss your hand, and I call you my queen.

KATHERINE Laissez, mon seigneur, laissez, laissez! Ma foi, je ne
veux point que vous abaissiez votre grandeur en baisant
la main d'une de votre seigneurie indigne serviteur.   250
Excusez-moi, je vous supplie, mon très-puissant
seigneur.[221]

KING Then I will kiss your lips, Kate.

KATHERINE Les dames et demoiselles pour être baisées devant leur
noces, il n'est pas la coutume de France.[222]

KING Madame, my interpreter, what says she?

ALICE Dat it is not be de fashion pour les ladies of France – I
cannot tell vat is baiser en Anglish.

KING To kiss.

ALICE Your majestee entend bettre que moi.[223]   260

KING It is not a fashion for the maids in France to kiss before
they are married, would she say?

ALICE	Oui, vraiment.[224]
KING	O Kate, nice customs curtsy to great kings. Dear Kate, you and I cannot be confined within the weak list of a country's fashion: we are the makers of manners, Kate; and the liberty that follows our places stops the mouth of all find-faults, as I will do yours, for upholding the nice fashion of your country, in denying me a kiss: therefore patiently, and yielding. [*He kisses her.*] 270 You have witchcraft in your lips, Kate: there is more eloquence in a sugar touch of them than in the tongues of the French Council; and they should sooner persuade Harry of England than a general petition of monarchs. Here comes your father.

The FRENCH KING *and* QUEEN *return with* BURGUNDY, EXETER,
WESTMORLAND, *and other French and English Lords.*

BURGUNDY	God save your Majesty! My royal cousin, teach you our princess English?
KING	I would have her learn, my fair cousin, how perfectly I love her, and that is good English.
BURGUNDY	Is she not apt? 280
KING	Our tongue is rough, coz, and my condition is not smooth: so that, having neither the voice nor the heart of flattery about me, I cannot so conjure up the spirit of love in her, that he will appear in his true likeness.
BURGUNDY	Pardon the frankness of my mirth, if I answer you for that. If you would conjure in her, you must make a circle;[225] if conjure up love in her in his true likeness, he must appear naked and blind.[226] Can you blame her then, being a maid yet rosed over with the virgin crimson of modesty, if she deny the appearance of a 290 naked blind boy in her naked seeing self? It were, my lord, a hard condition for a maid to consign to.
KING	Yet they do wink[227] and yield, as love is blind and enforces.
BURGUNDY	They are then excused, my lord, when they see not what they do.
KING	Then, good my lord, teach your cousin to consent winking.

BURGUNDY   I will wink on her to consent, my lord, if you will
           teach her to know my meaning: for maids, well   300
           summered and warm kept, are like flies at Bartholo-
           mew-tide, blind, though they have their eyes;[228] and
           then they will endure handling, which before would
           not abide looking on.

KING   This moral ties me over to time and a hot summer; and
           so I shall catch the fly, your cousin, in the latter end,[229]
           and she must be blind too.

BURGUNDY   As love is, my lord, before it loves.[230]

KING   It is so; and you may, some of you, thank love for my
           blindness, who cannot see many a fair French city for   310
           one fair French maid that stands in my way.

FR. KING   Yes, my lord, you see them perspectively:[231] the cities
           turned into a maid; for they are all girdled with maiden
           walls, that war hath never entered.

KING   Shall Kate be my wife?

FR. KING   So please you.

KING   I am content, so the maiden cities you talk of may wait
           on her: so the maid that stood in the way for my wish
           shall show me the way to my will.

FR. KING   We have consented to all terms of reason.   320

KING   Is't so, my lords of England?

WEST'LAND The King hath granted every article:
           His daughter first; and then in sequel all,
           According to their firm proposèd natures.

EXETER   Only he hath not yet subscribed this: Where your
           Majesty demands that the King of France, having
           any occasion to write for matter of grant, shall name
           your Highness in this form, and with this addition, in
           French: Notre très cher fils Henri, Roi d'Angleterre,
           Héritier de France;[232] and thus in Latin: Praeclarissimus   330
           filius noster Henricus Rex Angliae et Haeres
           Franciae.[233]

FR. KING   Nor this I have not, brother, so denied,
           But your request shall make me let it pass.

KING   I pray you then, in love and dear alliance,
           Let that one article rank with the rest,
           And thereupon give me your daughter.[234]

FR. KING   Take her, fair son, and from her blood raise up
           Issue to me, that the contending kingdoms
           Of France and England, whose very shores look pale   340
           With envy of each other's happiness,
           May cease their hatred; and this dear conjunction
           Plant neighbourhood and Christian-like accord
           In their sweet bosoms, that never war advance
           His bleeding sword 'twixt England and fair France.
ALL   Amen!
KING   Now welcome, Kate; and bear me witness all,
           That here I kiss her as my sovereign queen.   [*Flourish.*
ISABEL   God, the best maker of all marriages,
           Combine your hearts in one, your realms in one.   350
           As man and wife, being two, are one in love,
           So be there 'twixt your kingdoms such a spousal
           That never may ill office, or fell jealousy,
           Which troubles oft the bed of blessèd marriage,
           Thrust in between the paction of these kingdoms
           To make divorce of their incorporate league:
           That English may as French, French Englishmen,
           Receive each other. God speak this 'Amen'![235]
ALL   Amen!
KING   Prepare we for our marriage: on which day,   360
           My Lord of Burgundy, we'll take your oath,
           And all the peers', for surety of our leagues.
           Then shall I swear to Kate, and you to me,
           And may our oaths well kept and prosp'rous be!
                                              [*Sennet. Exeunt.*

EPILOGUE.

Enter CHORUS.

CHORUS   Thus far, with rough and all-unable pen,
           Our bending author hath pursued the story,
           In little room confining mighty men,
           Mangling by starts the full course of their glory.[236]
           Small time: but, in that small, most greatly lived
           This star of England. Fortune made his sword;
           By which the world's best garden he achieved,
           And of it left his son imperial lord.
           Henry the Sixth, in infant bands crowned King
           Of France and England, did this King succeed: 10
           Whose state so many had the managing,
           That they lost France, and made his England bleed:
           Which oft our stage hath shown;[237] and, for their sake,
           In your fair minds let this acceptance take.

NOTES ON *HENRY V*

In these notes, the following abbreviations are used:

F1: First Folio.

Holinshed: *Holinshed's Chronicles of England, Scotland, and Ireland* [1587] (London: Johnson *et al.*, 1807).

O.E.D.: *The Oxford English Dictionary* (London: Oxford University Press, 1933; rpt. 1961).

Q1: First Quarto.

Biblical quotations are from the Geneva Bible.

1 (1. Prologue, 9) *flat unraisèd spirits*: 'uninspired actors and playwright'.

2 (1. Prologue, 15–16) *may . . . million*: 'may concisely represent a million'.

3 (1. Prologue, 17) *ciphers . . . accompt*: 'mere noughts in this great account'.

4 (1.1.29) *th'offending Adam*: 'the sinfulness deriving from the disobedience of Adam'.

5 (1.1.46) *Gordian knot*: intricate knot devised by King Gordius. Alexander the Great cut it with his sword.

6 (1.1.48) *chartered libertine*: licensed freeman or sanctioned roamer.

7 (1.1.67) *miracles are ceased*: proverbial, but also a Protestant doctrine.

8 (1.1.89) *his great-grandfather*: King Edward III.

9 (1.2.11) *the law Salic*: This law excluded succession through the

female line. Henry's claim was based on his descent from Isabella, daughter of Philip IV of France and mother of Edward III of England.

10 (1.2.74) *Lingare*:   Holinshed's *Chronicles* (Shakespeare's main source for this play) gives 'Lingard'. The First Folio's 'Lingare' may be a misreading of Shakesepeare's handwriting, as the 'd' then could be mistaken for an 'e'.

11 (1.2.82) *Ermengare*:   Holinshed has 'Ermengard', so F1's 'Ermengare' may be a misreading.

12 (1.2.98) *Numbers*:   Chap. 27, verse 8.

13 (1.2.105–10) *Edward . . . nobility*:   At the battle of Cressy (Crécy), 1346, King Edward III refrained from sending reinforcements to his son, thus enabling that son, the Black Prince, to gain glory for this massive defeat of the French.

14 (1.2.119) *thrice-puissant*:   trebly powerful (perhaps because he is their heir, the monarch, and the inheritor of their spirit).

15 (1.2.161) *King of Scots*:   David II, captured in 1346.

16 (1.2.222) *Dolphin*:   This edition preserves the Elizabethan spelling, instead of modernising the word as 'Dauphin'.

17 (1.2.233) *Turkish mute*:   a Turkish slave whose tongue has been excised (perhaps to ensure that he says nothing of what he has observed in the harem).

18 (1.2.234) *waxen epitaph*:   ephemeral inscription, rather than one carved in stone or engraved in brass.

19 (2. Prologue, 7) *With wingèd . . . Mercuries*:   In Roman mythology, Mercury, messenger of the gods, had winged heels and a winged hat.

20 (2. Prologue, 32) *Th'abuse . . . play*:   F1 has 'Th'abuse of distance; force a play:', which is too short. I adopt Gary Taylor's emendation, so that the sense of the latter phrase becomes: 'and – necessarily – pack a play with incidents'.

21 (2. Prologue, 34–5) *the scene . . . Southampton*:   The next scene, however, takes place in London. Lines 41–2 seem to be an afterthought.

22 (2.1.32) *the prick of their needles*:   In performance, a slight pause after 'prick' can make evident the bawdry.

23 (2.1.34–6) *O well-a-day . . . committed*: 'Oh dear! By St Mary! He (Nym) has drawn his sword! If he is not wounded quickly (by Pistol), we shall see wilful adultery and murder committed!' Some editors emend F1's 'hewne' to 'here' or 'drawn'.

24 (2.1.39–40) *Iceland dog . . . cur of Iceland*: Icelandic dogs were reputed to be quarrelsome and 'prick-eared' (i.e. to have erect and pointed ears).

25 (2.1.43) *Will you . . . solus*: 'Will you move away? I intend to meet you alone.'

26 (2.1.50–51) *For I . . . follow*: 'For I can ignite: true to my name, I'm a cocked pistol, which will soon fire violently.' ('Pistol's cock is up' also has a bawdy sense.)

27 (2.1.69) *'Couple a gorge'*: garbled French for 'Cut the throat'.

28 (2.1.74) *lazar . . . kind*: 'leprous bird of prey of Cressida's kind', i.e. a prostitute. The legendary Cressida, unfaithful to Troilus, had been depicted as a leprous beggar by Robert Henryson.

29 (2.1.75) *Doll Tearsheet*: Falstaff's whore in *2 Henry IV*.

30 (2.1.76) *the quondam Quickly*: 'the former Quickly', now Pistol's wife.

31 (2.1.77) *my master*: Sir John Falstaff.

32 (2.1.85) *The King . . . heart*: by dismissing him (as dramatised in Act 5 of *2 Henry IV*).

33 (2.2.107–8) *Working . . . them*: 'collaborating so blatantly in a course natural to them that there was no astonished outcry'.

34 (2.2.142) *Another fall of man*: 'a new version of the Fall of Man' (see Genesis, Chapter 3). In *Richard II*, the deposition of Richard was described as 'a second fall of cursèd man'.

35 (2.2.157) *The sooner . . . intended*: Holinshed (Vol. 3, p. 71) says that Cambridge intended to help to the throne his brother-in-law, Edmund, Earl of March.

36 (2.3.9) *Arthur's bosom*: She means 'Abraham's bosom', heaven (see Luke 16:22).

37 (2.3.35) *Whore of Babylon*: the biblical 'great whore' and 'mother of whoredomes' (Geneva Bible: Revelation, Chap. 17).

38 (2.3.45) *Let . . . pay'*: 'Be governed by common sense. The motto should be: "Cash down; no credit".'

39 (2.3.48–9) *And Holdfast . . . counsellor*: 'The best guard–dog is the one called "Holdfast", my dear; therefore, let your adviser be "Beware".' (Keep a tight fist, and trust nobody.)

40 (2.3.50) *Go . . . crystals*: 'Go, wipe your (tearful) eyes.'

41 (2.3.56) *I cannot . . . of it*: because he still resents her marriage to Pistol.

42 (2.3.57) *Let . . . command*: 'Let good housekeeping be evident, and keep yourself to yourself, I command you.' 'Housewifery' was pronounced '*huzz*-if-ree'.

43 (2.4.4) *Britaine*: Brittany.

44 (2.4.5) *Orleance*: The word is spelt thus in Q1 and F1 (and in Holinshed). To modernise it as 'Orléans' would mar the metre.

45 (2.4.25) *Whitsun morris-dance*: Morris dancers traditionally performed (and perform) during the week of celebrations beginning on Whit Sunday, the seventh Sunday after Easter.

46 (2.4.37) *Roman Brutus*: the Brutus not of *Julius Caesar* but of *The Rape of Lucrece*. 'Brutus' is Latin for 'stupid'. Lucius Junius Brutus feigned stupidity as a protective guise; later he took revenge on Tarquin.

47 (2.4.57) *his mountain sire*: 'his father (King Edward III), as grandly immovable as a mountain'.

48 (2.4.99–100) *Therefore . . . Jove*: Jove cast thunderbolts at his enemies, and God deploys tempest, thunder and earthquake (Isaiah 29:7).

49 (2.4.102) *in . . . Lord*: 'in Christian fellowship' (Philippians 1:8).

50 (2.4.132) *Paris Louvre*: then the palace of French kings.

51 (2.4.137–8) *Now . . . grain*: 'Now he wastes no time, but values even the final grain (in the hour-glass).'

52 (3. Prologue, 4) *Dover pier*: F1 has 'Douer Peer'; some editors change this to 'Hampton pier', since elsewhere the text specifies Southampton as the departure-port. (Q1 lacks the speeches by 'Chorus'.)

53 (3. Prologue, 6) *With . . . fanning*: 'fanning with their silken pennants the rising sun'. (Phoebus Apollo was the sun-god.)

54 (3. Prologue, 21) *pith and puissance*:   'vigour and power'.

55 (3.1.19) *Alexanders*:   Alexander the Great (356–323 BC) led the Greeks to victory against the Persians.

56 (3.1.27) *The mettle of your pasture*:   'the quality of your land' (with a suggestion of 'metal').

57 (3.1.28) *worth your breeding*:   'worthy of your parentage and upbringing'.

58 (3.1.34) *Saint George*:   the patron saint of England, whose commemorative day (April 23rd) is regarded as Shakespeare's birthday.

59 (3.2.3–4) *The humour of it is too hot*:   'the nature of it (the military action) is too dangerous'. Elsewhere in this scene, 'humours' means mainly 'passions, sentiments or attitudes'.

60 (3.2.24–5) *These . . . bad humours*:   'Pistol is expressing good sentiments. You, your honour, gain my disapproval.' Some editors change 'wins' to 'runs', so that the meaning of the second sentence is (more or less) 'Your honour is behaving badly.'

61 (3.2.44) *carry coals*:   tolerate insults.

62 (3.2.58–9) *is digt . . . countermines*:   F1 has 'is digt himselfe foure yard vnder the Countermines'. I adopt the punctuation of Gary Taylor's Oxford edition, to yield the correct sense: 'has dug countermines which are four yards beneath our mines'.

63 (3.2.60) *plow up all*:   'blow everything up' (by detonating explosives beneath the British tunnels).

64 (3.2.82) *By Chrish, law*:   'Law' is an intensifier of oaths, corresponding approximately to 'so I swear!'; it was sometimes spelt 'la'.

65 (3.2.96–7) *I sall . . . leve*:   'I shall requite you, with your kind permission'.

66 (3.2.109) *Ay owe God a death*:   F1 has 'ay, or goe to death', but the context supports the emendation.

67 (3.2.115–16) *Ish a villain . . . rascal?*:   'Because I'm Irish, are you about to heap insults upon me?'

68 (3.3.26–7) *As send . . . ashore*: cf. Job 40:20: 'Canst thou draw
    out Liuiathan with an hooke . . . ?' ('Liuiathan' – Leviathan – is
    the whale, according to the Geneva Bible's marginal gloss.)

69 (3.3.40–41) *as did the wives . . . slaughtermen*: Matthew 2:16–
    18. King Herod ordered the murder of all the children in the
    Bethlehem area who were two years old or less than two.
    There ensued 'mourning, and weping, and great lamentation:
    Rachel weping for her children'.

70 (3.3.54) *Use . . . uncle*: F1 has: 'Vse mercy to them all for vs,
    deare Vnckle': i.e. 'On my behalf, treat them mercifully, dear
    uncle'. Some editors emend the line thus: 'Use mercy to them
    all. For us, dear uncle'. (Holinshed says that the town was
    sacked and its inhabitants expelled.)

71 (Act 3, scene 4). The French in this scene is sometimes
    incorrect or archaic. Kate's language-lesson culminates in two
    obscene puns. These, and various errors, are noted subse-
    quently. For now, here is a translation:

    Katherine: 'Alice, you have been in England, and you speak the
    language well.' Alice: 'A little, madam.' Katherine: 'I beg you,
    teach me: I must learn to speak it. How do you say "la main" in
    English?' Alice: ' "La main"? It is called "de hand".' Katherine:
    ' "De hand". And "les doigts"?' Alice: ' "Les doigts"? Bless my
    soul! I forget "les doigts"; but I shall remember. "Les doigts"? I
    think that they are called "de fingrès"; yes, "de fingrès".'
    Katherine: ' "La main", "de hand"; "les doigts", "de fingrès". I
    think I am a good pupil. I have quickly acquired two words of
    English. What are "les ongles" called?' Alice: ' "Les ongles?" We
    call them "de nails".' Katherine: ' "De nails". Listen: tell me if I
    say it well: "de hand", "de fingrès", and "de nails".' Alice: 'Well
    spoken, madam; it is very good English.' Katherine: 'Tell me the
    English for "le bras".' Alice: ' "De arma", madam.' Katherine:
    'And "le coude".' Alice: ' "D'elbow".' Katherine: ' "D'elbow".
    I shall repeat all the words you have taught me up to now.'
    Alice: 'That is too difficult, madam, in my opinion.' Katherine:
    'Excuse me, Alice; listen: "d'hand". "de fingrè", "de nails",
    "d'arma", "de bilbow".' Alice: ' "D'elbow", madam.' Katherine:
    'Oh, Lord! I'm forgetting it! "D'elbow". How do you say "le
    col"?' Alice: ' "De nick", madam.' Katherine: ' "De nick". And

"le menton"?' Alice: ' "De chin".' Katherine: ' "De sin". "Le col", "de nick"; "le menton", "de sin".' Alice: 'Yes. Saving your honour [i.e. with respect, without offence to your honour]: truly, you pronounce the words as correctly as do the natives of England.' Katherine: 'I have no doubt at all that I shall learn, by the grace of God, and in a short time.' Alice: 'Haven't you already forgotten what I have taught you?' Katherine: 'No; I shall immediately repeat to you: "d'hand", "de fingrè", "de mailès" – ' Alice: ' "De nails", madam.' Katherine: ' "De nails", "de arm", "de ilbow" – ' Alice: ' "With respect: "d'elbow".' Katherine: 'That's what I'm saying – "d'elbow"; "de nick" and "de sin". What do you call "le pied" and "la robe"?' Alice: 'The "foot", madam, and the "coun".' Katherine: 'The "foot", and the "coun"? Oh Lord! These words sound bad, corruptive, gross and shameless, and not to be used by well-bred ladies: I would not, for all the world, utter these words in front of French noblemen. Ugh! The "foot" and the "coun"! Nevertheless, I shall once more recite the entire lesson: "d'hand", "de fingrè", "de nails", "d'arm", "d'elbow", "de nick", "de sin", "de foot", the "coun".' Alice: 'Excellent, madam!' Katherine: 'That is enough for now. Let us go to dinner.'

72 (3.4.1) *tu . . . langage*:   i.e. (correctly or preferably today), 'tu parles bien la langue'.

73 (3.4.3) *Je . . . m'enseignez*:   i.e. 'Je te prie de m'enseigner'.

74 (3.4.11) *je suis . . . écolier*:   i.e. 'je suis une bonne écolière (*or* élève)'.

75 (3.4.16) *il est . . . anglais*:   i.e. 'c'est du fort bon anglais'.

76 (3.4.21) *Je m'en . . . répétition*:   i.e. 'Je fais la répétition'.

77 (3.4.28) *je m'en oublie!*:   i.e. 'j'oublie!'.

78 (3.4.34) *droit*:   i.e. 'correctement'.

79 (3.4.38) *je réciterai à vous*:   i.e. 'je vais vous réciter'.

80 (3.4.46) *Le foot, et le coun?*:   Katherine is understandably shocked by these words. To her, 'foot' sounds like the French 'foutre', which, as a noun, means 'semen' (and, as a verb, obscenely means 'to fuck'). 'Coun' (Alice's version of 'gown') sounds to her like the French noun 'con', which corresponds to the English obscene term 'cunt'. Q1 gives not 'coun' but

'con'; and, in the Olivier film, that is how the embarrassed Princess said it.

81 (3.4.46) *Ils sont mots*:   i.e. 'Ce sont des mots'

82 (3.4.47–8) *non pour . . . d'user*:   i.e. 'que les dames honorables (*or* honnêtes) ne doivent pas employer'.

83 (3.4.50–1) *je réciterai une autre fois*:   i.e. 'je vais réciter encore une fois'.

84 (3.4.55) *allons-nous à dîner*:   i.e. 'allons dîner'.

85 (3.5.5) *O Dieu vivant!*:   'O living God!'

86 (3.5.5–9) *Shall . . . grafters?*:   'Shall a few French shoots, the discharge of our (Norman) ancestors' lust, offshoots grafted to wild and savage (English) stock, sprout up so suddenly into the clouds and look down on those who did the grafting?'

87 (3.5.11) *Mort de ma vie!*:   'Death of my life!'

88 (3.5.15) *Dieu de batailles!*:   'God of battles!'

89 (3.5.25) *Sweat . . . fields!*:   'scatter on our rich fields drops of sweat from their gallant young men!'

90 (3.5.26) *Poor . . . lords*:   'Our fields should properly be called not rich but poor, since their French owners set such poor examples.'

91 (3.5.52) *void his rheum*:   'discharge his phlegm'.

92 (3.5.54) *captive chariot*:   chariot for displaying captured enemies.

93 (3.6.4) *bridge*:   In Fluellen's speeches as represented in F1, 'bridge' first appears twice as 'bridge' but thereafter as 'pridge'.

94 (3.6.6–7) *Agamemnon*:   the Greek war-lord who led the Greek armies to the siege and sack of Troy. George Puttenham in 1589 referred to his 'magnanimity'.

95 (3.6.14) *Mark Antony*:   the Roman warrior who fought (and was defeated by) Octavius Caesar.

96 (3.6.39) *pax*:   a tablet, bearing a sacred image, kissed by the priest and others present during the Mass.

97 (3.6.81) *find a hole in his coat*:   'have an opportunity to expose him'.

98 (3.6.98–9) *bubukles and whelks*:   A bubo is a glandular swelling or abscess, and a carbuncle is a boil, pimple, inflamed ulcer or tumour. Fluellen conflates the two names. Whelks are pimples.

99 (3.6.121) *admire our sufferance*: 'wonder at our (previous) forbearance'.

100 (3.6.154) *There's . . . Montjoy*:   Holinshed says that Henry gave Montjoy 'a princely reward'.

101 (3.7.12) *Ça*:   'That one'.

102 (3.7.13) *as if . . . hairs*:   Tennis-balls were stuffed with hair. (An alternative reading is 'as if his entrails were hares'.)

103 (3.7.13–14) *le cheval . . . feu*:   Translation: 'the flying horse, the Pegasus, who has fiery nostrils'. Pegasus is the winged horse of Greek mythology, and is associated with poetic genius.

104 (3.7.17) *more musical . . . Hermes*:   The god Hermes charmed Argus to sleep by playing his pipe.

105 (3.7.19) *Perseus*:   Renaissance poets said that Perseus rode Pegasus when rescuing Andromeda.

106 (3.7.20–21) *he is . . . in him*:   Earth, water, air and fire were regarded as the four constituent elements of the world, the last two being associated with aspiration and transcendence.

107 (3.7.50–51) *like a kern . . . strossers*:   'like an Irish peasant, in clinging breeches instead of your baggy French ones'. ('Strait strossers' are tight trousers. Some editors speculate that the phrase refers jocularly to bare legs. 'Clinging breeches' suit the equestrian and amatory contexts.)

108 ((3.7.54) *foul bogs*:   (a) Irish bogs; (b) the anal region.

109 (3.7.60–61) *'Le chien . . . bourbier'*:   Proverbial, from 2 Peter 2:22: 'The dogge is returned to his owne vomit: and, The sowe that was washed, to the wallowing in the myer.'

110 (3.7.86) *tread . . . oath*:   'rub it out with her foot'.

111 (3.7.88) *still be doing*:   (a) 'constantly be in action'; (b) 'never stop copulating'.

112 (3.7.99–100) *'tis . . . bate*:   A tame falcon was hooded until ready for flight; then the hood was removed and it would 'bate' (flutter its wings). The Constable puns: 'bate' could also mean 'abate, diminish'.

113 (3.7.110–11) *You have . . . overshot*:   'You have overshot the target.' 'It is not the first time you were overshot.' 'Overshot'

means successively (a) 'missed', (b) 'wide of the mark your-self', and possibly (c) 'intoxicated'.

114 (3.7.120–21) *to mope . . . knowledge*: 'to wander with his thick-witted followers so far into perils he fails to comprehend'.

115 (3.7.130) *Russian bear*:   as used in a bear-baiting ring.

116 (4. Prologue, 39–40) *over-bears . . . semblance*: 'subdues weariness by his cheerful appearance'.

117 (4.1.12) *make a moral of*:   'draw a moral lesson from'.

118 (4.1.19) *upon example*:   'by imitating the good conduct of others'.

119 (4.1.35) *Qui vous là?*:   'Who are you there?'. F1 has '*Che vous la?*', which some editors emend to '*Qui va là?*' ('Who goes there?').

120 (4.1.42) *the Emperor*:   Sigismund, the Holy Roman Emperor.

121 (4.1.49) *le Roy*:   'the King'.

122 (4.1.51) *a Welshman*:   born at Monmouth.

123 (4.1.55) *Saint Davy's day*:   The leek is a Welsh national emblem, and the commemorative day of St David, patron saint of Wales, is March 1st.

124 (4.1.104–5) *they stoop . . . wing*:   a metaphor from falconry again. 'Stoop' means 'swoop'.

125 (4.1.132) *latter day*:   Doomsday, the Day of Judgement.

126 (4.1.140–41) *against . . . subjection*: 'contrary to the proper relationship between sovereign and subject'.

127 (4.1.189–90) *You pay . . . elder-gun*: 'You punish him then! That's no more dangerous than a missile from a pea-shooter'.

128 (4.1.215) *crowns*:   (a) gold coins; (b) heads.

129 (4.1.217–18) *no English . . . crowns*:   In England, to clip the edges from gold coins was a treasonable offence.

130 (4.1.229) *ceremony*:   pomp, display and the trappings of power.

131 (4.1.253) *farcèd . . . King*:   'stuffed (bombastic) epithets preceding the King's name' (e.g. 'His Majesty').

132 (4.1.263–5) *Phoebus . . . Elysium . . . Hyperion*: Phoebus Apollo

is the sun-god, so here 'Phoebus' equals the sun; Elysium is
the abode of bliss in the classical Underworld; and 'Hyperion'
(the heroic Titan) is regarded by Shakespeare as another sun-
god.

133 (4.1.274) *Whose . . . advantages*: 'whose hours of vigilance
most benefit the peasant'.

134 (4.1.283–4) *the fault . . . crown*: Henry's father, Bolingbroke,
had become King Henry IV after deposing King Richard II,
who was then murdered.

135 (4.2.2) *Montez . . . Ha!*: 'To horse! My horse! Groom!
Lackey! Ha!' ('Montez à cheval!' is correct, though a more
likely military command would be 'En selle!')

136 (4.2.4) *Via! . . . terre!*: 'Away! Water and earth!'

137 (4.2.5) *Rien . . . feu?*: 'Nothing afterwards? Air and fire?'

138 (4.2.6) *Cieux*: 'Heavens'.

139 (4.2.35) *the tucket . . . mount*: 'the resonant trumpet-call and
the signal to mount'.

140 (4.2.41) *curtains*: here, 'banners'.

141 (4.2.43) *Big Mars*: mighty Mars, the god of war.

142 (4.2.60) *I . . . guidon*: 'I am waiting for my pennant only'.

143 (4.3.14) *framed . . . valour*: 'composed of firm and constant
valour'.

144 (4.3.39) *That . . . us*: 'who fears to die in company with me'.

145 (4.3.40) *feast of Crispian*: October 25th, the feast-day of
Saints Crispin (or Crispinus) and Crispinian (or Crispianus),
two brothers from Rome who were said to have lived as
missionaries at Soissons in France and to have been martyred
there around AD 287. One English tradition claims that they
actually fled to Faversham in Kent and worked there as
cobblers, subsequently being commemorated in the parish
church; another claims that after the martyrdom in France,
their bodies were cast into the sea and floated ashore at
Romney Marsh.

146 (4.3.57) *Crispin Crispian*: i.e. the feast-day of Saints
Crispinus and Crispianus.

147 (4.3.105) *like . . . crazing*: 'like the fragments flying from shattered cannon-balls'.

148 (4.3.107) *in . . . mortality*: 'when falling back into death'.

149 (4.4.2) *Je . . . qualité*: 'I think that you are a high-ranking gentleman.' ('Le gentilhomme' should correctly be 'un gentilhomme'.)

150 (4.4.3) *Calen . . . me*: an Elizabethan version of an Irish refrain meaning 'Maiden, my treasure'.

151 (4.4.5) *O . . . Dieu!*: 'Oh, Lord God!'

152 (4.4.11) *O . . . moi!*: 'Oh, show mercy! Have pity on me!' (Modern French would prefer 'ayez miséricorde' to 'prenez miséricorde.) 'Moi' here evidently rhymes with 'boy'.

153 (4.4.12) *Moy*: Pistol apparently takes a 'moy' to be a coin.

154 (4.4.13) *fetch thy rim*: 'drag your guts' ('rim' being the peritoneum, the membrane covering the abdomen).

155 (4.4.15) *Est-il . . . bras?*: 'Is it impossible to escape the strength of your arm?' (In F1, the equivalent of 'd'échapper à la force' is 'd'eschapper le force'.)

156 (4.4.16) *Brass, cur?*: The s of 'bras' would have been sounded in 16th-century French: hence Pistol's misunderstanding. 'Brass' could mean 'coins of low value'.

157 (4.4.19) *O . . . moi!*: 'Oh, spare me!'

158 (4.4.23) *Écoutez . . . appelé?*: 'Listen: what is your name?' (Correctly, not 'comment êtes-vous appelé?' but 'comment vous appelez-vous?')

159 (4.4.26) *I'll fer . . . ferret him*: probably: 'I'll put fear into him, and beat him, and tear at him'.

160 (4.4.30) *Que . . . monsieur?*: 'What is he saying, sir?'

161 (4.4.31–3) *Il . . . gorge*: 'He orders me to tell you that you should prepare yourself, for this soldier here is inclined to cut your throat promptly.' ('À vous dire que vous faites vous prêt' and 'de couper' would be better French as 'de vous dire que vous devez vous apprêter' and 'à couper'.

162 (4.4.34) *Oui . . . foi*: 'Yes, cut the throat, by my faith'.

163 (4.4.37–9) *O . . . écus*: 'Oh, I beseech you, for the love of God, spare me! I am a gentleman of good family: preserve my

life, and I will give you two hundred crowns.' ('Me pardonnez' and 'le gentilhomme' should be 'de me pardonner' and 'un gentilhomme'.)

164 (4.4.46) *Petit . . . dit-il?*: 'Little gentleman, what does he say?'

165 (4.4.47–50) *Encore . . . franchisement.*: 'Again, that to spare any prisoner is contrary to his oath; nevertheless, in return for the crowns that you promise him, he is willing to grant you liberty, freedom.' (His 'qu'il est' and 'à vous' should rather be 'que c'est' and 'de vous'.)

166 (4.4.51–4) *Sur . . . d'Angleterre*: 'On my knees, I give you a thousand thanks, and I regard myself as fortunate to have fallen into the hands of a knight whom I deem the most brave, valiant and highly distinguished nobleman of England.'

167 (4.4.61) *Suivez-vous . . . capitaine!*: 'Follow the great captain!' (The '-vous' is redundant.)

168 (4.4.65–6) *this . . . dagger*: 'this fellow, who not only roars like the Devil in old Morality plays, but can also be fooled by anyone, as the Devil was when the Vice in the play pared his claws'.

169 (4.5.1–3) *O . . . vie!*: 'Oh, the devil!' 'Oh, Lord! The day is lost, everything is lost!' 'Death of my life!'

170 (4.5.6) *O . . . fortune!*: 'Oh, wicked Fortune!'

171 (4.5.12) *Let . . . again*: F1 gives 'Let vs dye in once more backe againe'. I have emended it to restore the metre. Other editors suggest 'Let us die instant. Once more back again' and 'Let us die in arms: once more back again'.

172 (4.6.31) *my mother . . . eyes*: 'the tenderness inherited from my mother filled my eyes'.

173 (4.6.33–4) *compound . . . eyes*: 'come to terms with my moist eyes' (presumably by wiping them).

174 (4.6.37) *Then . . . prisoners*: Here the order to kill the prisoners is a response to a rally by the French forces; yet, in Act 4, scene 7, the order is regarded as a response to a raid by French runaways on the boys and the King's tent. Gary Taylor's edition adds a direction that prisoners be killed on stage, but

Henry's 'Give the word through' ('Pass the order on') makes
this unlikely.

175 (4.7.1) *Kill the poys and the luggage!*:   i.e. 'Kill the boys and
plunder the baggage!'

176 (4.7.33) *Cleitus*:   Alexander, in a drunken rage, killed his
faithful friend, Cleitus.

177 (4.7.54–5) *stones . . . slings*:   Apocrypha: Judith 9:7: '[T]he
Assyrians . . . trust in shield, speare and bowe, and sling'.

178 (4.7.85) *grandfather*:   Edward III was the great-grandfather of
Henry V.

179 (4.7.101–2) *His . . . majesty too!*:   'His' is capitalised here
(twice), as it refers to God. (In contrast, Fluellen says '*your*
Majesty' when referring to the King.)

180 (4.7.126–7) *quite . . . degree*:   'far above the obligation to re-
spond to a challenge from such an inferior person'.

181 (4.7.128) *as good . . . devil is*:   cf.: 'The Prince of Darkness is
a gentleman' (*King Lear*, Act 3, scene 4).

182 (4.7.129) *Lucifer . . . Belzebub*:   Lucifer ('Light-bearer'), the
brightest of the angels, fell and became Satan; Belzebub (or
Beelzebub), 'Lord of the Flies', is a subordinate devil.

183 (4.8.118) *'Non nobis' and 'Te Deum'*:   Holinshed (Vol. 3, p.
82) says that Henry told the priests 'to sing this psalme: In exitu
Israel de Aegypto [114, "When Israel came out of Egypt"], and
commanded euerie man to kneele downe on the ground at this
verse: Non nobis Domine, non nobis, sed nomini tuo da
gloriam [now the opening of Psalm 115 of the *Book of Common
Prayer*: "Not unto us, O Lord, not unto us, but unto thy Name
give the praise"]. Which doone, he caused Te Deum . . . to be
soong . . . ' (The 'Te Deum' is a famous canticle; the opening,
'Te deum laudamus', means 'We praise thee, O God'.)

184 (5. Prologue, 16) *Blackheath*:   an expanse of open ground,
south-east of London.

185 (5. Prologue, 23) *In the . . . thought*:   'in thought's lively
smithy and workshop': i.e. in your imagination.

186 (5. Prologue, 30) *the General . . . Empress*:   Robert Devereux,
Earl of Essex, had set out from London on 27 March 1599 to

suppress an insurrection in Ireland. He failed, incurring the enmity of the 'gracious Empress', Queen Elizabeth, and arrived back in London on 28 September.

187 (5. Prologue, 38) *The Emperor's coming*:   Holinshed reports that the Holy Roman Emperor, Sigismund, came to England in a futile endeavour to reconcile Henry V and Charles VI.

188 (5. Prologue, 39) *them*:   In F1, some words may be missing between 'them:' and 'and omit'. One editor suggests: '— But these now / We pass in silence over;'.

189 (5.1.18–19) *Art thou . . . web?*:   'Are you insane? Do you, low foreigner, seek death at my hands?' In classical mythology, the Parcae are the three Fates who spin, draw out and cut the thread of life. Pistol thinks of one Fate who makes a 'web' (woven cloth) of life.

190 (5.1.26) *Cadwallader . . . goats*:   According to chroniclers, Cadwallader was the last of the British kings, dying at Rome in 689. It was said that in his reign, the Saxons gained much of Britain, and the British took refuge in Wales. After his day, the British would be called 'Welsh' ('Foreign'). Shakespeare associates Wales with mountain-goats.

191 (5.1.59) *in . . . revenge*:   'as a pledge that revenge has been incurred'.

192 (5.1.69–70) *gleeking . . . gentleman*:   'mocking and irritating the gentleman'.

193 (5.1.76) *Doth . . . now?*:   'Does the goddess Fortune treat me now as if she were a hussy [a fickle woman]?'

194 (5.1.77) *my Doll is dead*:   Pistol is married to Nell Quickly, whose name is here confused with that of Doll Tearsheet.

195 (5.1.78) *malady of France*:   venereal disease.

196 (5.2.12) *England*:   F1 has 'Ireland'.

197 (5.2.15–17) *your eyes . . . basilisks*:   'your eyeballs have hitherto, in their aim against the French who encountered them, been as deadly not only as those of murderous serpents but also as the balls fired by murderous cannon'. ('Basilisk' was originally the name of a mythical serpent whose eyes could kill, and subsequently the name of a large cannon.)

198 (5.2.39) *her husbandry . . . heaps*: 'her agricultural produce lies in heaps'.

199 (5.2.82–3) *suddenly . . . answer*: 'speedily pronounce our agreed and final response'.

200 (5.2.108) *Pardonnez-moi*: 'Pardon me'.

201 (5.2.110–11) *Que dit-il . . . dit-il*: 'What does he say — that I resemble angels?' 'Yes, truly (saving your grace): so he says.' (I emend F1's 'à les' as 'aux'.)

202 (5.2.114–15) *O . . . tromperies*: 'Oh, good Lord! Men's tongues are full of deception'.

203 (5.2.120) *The Princess . . . Englishwoman*: because she will appreciate the King's plain utterances.

204 (5.2.130) *Sauf . . . honneur*: 'Saving your honour'.

205 (5.2.133–5) *nor measure . . . strength*: 'Measure' means successively: (a) metre, (b) dance-steps, and (c) allocation.

206 (5.2.137) *under . . . spoken*: 'at the risk of being rebuked for bragging'.

207 (5.2.138) *leap into*: (a) gain; (b) enter sexually.

208 (5.2.148–9) *let . . . cook*: 'let your vision improve the spectacle, as a cook improves the ingredients'.

209 (5.2.178–80) *Je . . . moi*: 'I, when I have the ownership of France, and when you own me'. ('Le possession' should correctly be '*la* possession'. I emend F1's 'sur' as 'j'ai'.)

210 (5.2.180–81) *Saint . . . speed!*: 'May St Denis, the patron saint of France, help me!'

211 (5.2.181–2) *donc . . . mienne*: 'then France is yours, and you are mine'.

212 (5.2.185–6) *Sauf . . . parle*: 'Saving your honour, the French that you speak is better than the English that I speak.'

213 (5.2.200) *I get . . . scambling*: 'I shall have won you by fighting a war'.

214 (5.2.204–5) *go to . . . beard?*: i.e. retrieve Constantinople for Christendom (though the Turks did not capture Constantinople until 1453, 31 years after Henry's death).

215 (5.2.206) *flower-de-luce*: the fleur-de-lis (lily flower), the French royal emblem.

216 (5.2.212–13) *la plus . . . déesse*: 'the most beautiful Katherine in the world, my very dear and divine goddess'. (In the French, the later words should correctly be 'ma très chère et divine déesse').

217 (5.2.214) *fausse*: (correctly 'faux':) (a) incorrect; (b) deceptive.

218 (5.2.215) *sage demoiselle*: 'wise (*or* prudent) young lady'.

219 (5.2.236) *Plantagenet*: The Plantagenets were a dynasty of kings established in 1154 with the reign of Henry II.

220 (5.2.243) *de roi mon père*: 'the King, my father'.

221 (5.2.248–52) *Laissez . . . seigneur*: 'Stop, my lord, stop, stop! By my faith, I do not in the least wish you to abase your majesty by kissing the hand of an unworthy servant of your lordship. Excuse me, I beg you, my very powerful lord.' ('D'une . . . serviteur' should preferably be 'd'un . . . serviteur' or 'd'une . . . servante'.)

222 (5.2.254–5) *Les dames . . . France*: 'In France, it is not the custom for ladies and young ladies to be kissed before their weddings.' (Her phrasing should preferably be: 'Pour les dames et demoiselles d'être baisées avant leur noces, ce n'est pas la coutume de France.' The verb 'baiser' connotes copulation and not merely kissing.)

223 (5.2.260) *Your . . . moi*: 'Your Majesty understands better than I.'

224 (5.2.263) *Oui, vraiment*: 'Yes, truly.'

225 (5.2.286–7) *make a circle*: (a) make a magician's circle; (b) open her vulva.

226 (5.2.288) *naked and blind*: (a) like Cupid, the naked and blindfolded love-god; (b) like the penis.

227 (5.2.293) *wink*: here, 'close both eyes', but, at line 299, 'give the wink' in the modern sense.

228 (5.2.300–302) *maids . . . eyes*: 'maidens, pampered and cosseted, are like sun-heated flies on St Bartholomew's Day (August 24th): though they have eyes, they are blinded by sexual desire'. (*O.E.D.* shows that 'blind', in such phrases as 'blind appetite of lust', can mean 'rendered reckless and undiscriminating by sexual desire'. This sense is used at 3.3.34. Shakespeare repeatedly associates flies with lechery.)

229 (5.2.306) *in the latter end*:   (a) in late summer; (b) by her lower end.

230 (5.2.308) *As . . . loves*:   'As love is, my lord, prior to physical love-making.' (Gary Taylor emends the latter part of the line to 'before that it loves'.)

231 (5.2.312) *perspectively*:   as in an artefact which yields one image (or a confused image) when seen from one angle and another (or a clear image) when seen from a different angle.

232 (5.2.329–30) *Notre . . . France*:   'Our very dear son, Henry, King of England, Heir of France'.

233 (5.2.330–2) *Praeclarissimus . . . Franciae*:   'Our most renowned son, Henry, King of England and Heir of France'.

234 (5.2.337) *And . . . daughter*:   This line is oddly unmetrical in F1, too. A gesturing actor could supply a silent iambic foot between 'thereupon' and 'give', or 'daughter' could be emended to 'daughter's hand'.

235 (5.2.358) *God . . . 'Amen'!*:   'To this injunction, may God declare "Let it be so"!'

236 (Epilogue, 4) *Mangling . . . glory*:   'erratically marring the full progress of their glorious careers'.

237 (Epilogue, 13) *Which . . . shown*:   in Shakespeare's three plays on the disastrous reign of Henry VI. This closing sonnet thus turns a sequence of history plays into a cycle.

GLOSSARY

Where a pun or ambiguity is intended, the meanings are distinguished as (a) and (b). Otherwise, alternative meanings are distinguished as (i) and (ii). The following abbreviations are used: adj., adjective; adv., adverb; *O.E.D.*, *Oxford English Dictionary*; S.D., Stage Direction; vb., verb.

a (as pronoun): he.
absolute: perfect.
accomplish: equip completely.
accord (vb.): agree, consent.
achieve: (i) gain; (ii) end.
act of order: orderly practice.
addition: title, style of address.
admiration: wonder, astonishment.
admire (vb.): wonder at.
advantage (noun): (i) favourable opportunity; (ii) embellishment.
adventures, at all: whatever be the consequences.
affections: desires.
affiance: trust.
alarum: trumpet-call to arms.
Albion: the island consisting of England, Wales and Scotland (3.5.14).
ale-washed: ale-fuddled.
amen: 'so let it be'; certainly.
ample: complete.

amply: frankly.
Ancient: ensign, standard-bearer; equivalent to sub-lieutenant in recent times.
annoy: hurt.
anon: at once, very soon.
answer (noun): penalty, satisfaction.
answer (vb.): (i) answer for (4.1.150); (ii) match (4. Prologue, 8).
an't: if it.
antique (noun): old person (with hint of 'antic', buffoon: 3.2.29).
antique (adj.): ancient.
apace: quickly.
approbation: attestation.
argument: subject-matter, business in hand.
art: skill (1.1.51).
Arthur's bosom: heaven.
assay: assault.
astonish: stun (5.1.37).

attaint: exhaustion, staleness.

attend (on): wait upon; accompany.

attest: (i) represent; (ii) vouch for; (iii) prove.

avaunt: go forward.

awkward: perverse.

ay (as pronoun): I.

ay, aye (as adv.): yes.

bands: swaddling-clothes (Epilogue, 9).

bankrout: bankrupt.

bar: court of decision (5.2.27).

Barbason: supposedly the name of a devil; perhaps a confusion of 'Barbas' (name of a devil) with 'Barbason' (name of a French knight whose resistance to Henry is described by Holinshed).

barley broth: strong ale.

base: low-born.

basilisk: (a) mythical serpent whose stare could kill; (b) cannon.

bate: flutter.

battle: line, battle-array, army.

bawcock: fine fellow.

bawd: pimp.

bear: (i) perform (1.2.213); (ii) carry.

beaver: visor.

become: grace, adorn (1.2.8, 3.1.3).

bedlam (adj.): mad.

bend up: strain to the utmost.

bent (noun): aim.

beshrew: curse.

blind: filled with indiscriminate sexual lust (3.3.34, 5.2.302).

blown from: (a) puffed from, (b) inflated by (4.1.244).

bolted: sifted (2.2.137).

bonnet: cap, headgear.

book (vb.): record.

boot: booty; **make boot upon**: plunder.

bottoms: hulls of ships, or ships themselves.

bow (vb.): bend; falsify.

brave: fine, gallant.

breath: breathing-time, brief interval (2.4.145).

bred out: exhausted, degenerated.

Britaine: Brittany.

broached: spitted.

broken music: (a) music arranged in parts, (b) faulty utterance.

brook (vb.): bear.

bruise an injury: squeeze a boil.

bubukle: a conflation of 'bubo' (glandular swelling or abscess) and 'carbuncle' (boil, pimple, inflamed ulcer, or tumour).

bully: fine fellow.

burnet: low-growing flowering plant.

butt: target.

Cadwallader: last British king (when the Britons had retreated to Wales).

Callice: Calais.

capital (adj.): principal (5.2.97).

careful: full of cares; anxious.

carry coals: submit tamely to insults as if one were the lowest of menials.

case: set.
casques: helmets.
cause: matter, affair.
Caveto (Latin): caution; beware.
celerity: speed.
ceremony: trappings or symbols of power.
challenge: lay claim to.
chamber: gun for use in theatre (3. Prologue 33, S.D.).
change (vb.): lose colour (2.2.73).
change, in: in exchange.
charge (noun): duty (4.3.6).
charm (vb.): command by magic.
chartered: privileged, licensed.
chase: (a) missed return, (b) pursuit.
chaw: chew.
cherish: favour.
chewed: ruminated, pondered.
chivalry: men at arms.
choice-drawn: (a) selected with care, (b) voluntary.
christom: innocent. (A 'christom child' was one that died soon after its christening.)
chuck: chick (term of endearment).
clap hands: strike hands to seal a bargain.
clipper: one who pares coins.
close (noun): (a) cadence, (b) close union.
close (vb.): meet, unite.
close (adv.): in privacy.
cockpit: (i) arena for cock-fighting; (ii) disparaging term for a theatre.
come over: reproach, deride.
comings-in: revenues, income.

companies: companions (1.1.55).
complement: (i) outward bearing or appearance; (ii) accomplishments, personal qualities.
compound: come to terms.
con: memorise.
condition: (i) quality, disposition, character; (ii) rank.
confirm: ratify.
confounded: worn away; ruined, lost.
congree: mutually agree.
congreet: greet each other.
conjuration: solemn appeal.
conscience: real opinion, conviction (4.1.114, 4.7.133).
consent: (i) (a) unanimity, (b) playing or singing together (1.2.181, 2.2.22); (ii) concerted plan of action (1.2.206).
consideration: reflection.
consign: agree.
contagious: pestilential.
controversy: struggle.
conveyed himself: passed himself off.
convoy: conveyance.
copy: example.
coranto: swift dance.
correct (vb.): impose penalties (1.2.191).
correction: punishment.
corroborate: strengthened (used inappropriately at 2.1.120).
couch: crouch, cower.
coulter: iron cutter at the front of a ploughshare.

courser: charger; large, swift
   horse.
coursing: marauding.
coz: familiar form of 'cousin'.
crazing: shattering.
create: made, composed
   (2.2.31).
crescive in its faculty: growing
   according to its nature.
Crispin Crispian: the feast-day
   of Saints Crispin (Crispinus)
   and Crispinian (Crispianus),
   Oct. 25th.
crown: (i) (a) gold coin, (b)
   head; (ii) monarch's crown.
cry out: complain loudly or
   vehemently.
culled: selected.
cullion: rascal, wretch.
currence, heady: strong flow.
cursitory: cursory.
curtle-axe: short broad-sword,
   cutlass.

dare the field: (a) defy the
   enemy, (b) paralyse the
   opposition (4.2.36).
darnel: rye-grass.
dear: (i) considerate (2.2.58);
   (ii) dire, grievous (2.2.181).
decoct: cook, boil.
deracinate: uproot.
despite: contempt.
diffused: disorderly.
digest: accommodate, accept.
discuss: declare.
dishonest: unchaste.
divers: (a) sundry, (b) diverse.
dout: douse, extinguish.
down-roping: falling in long
   strings.

drench: medicinal draught or
   'mash' for horses.
dress: prepare (4.1.10).
duke: leader (3.2.22).

egregious: exceptional, extra-
   ordinary.
elder-gun: pea-shooter.
element: sky.
embassy: mission.
empery: sovereignty.
englutted: swallowed up.
enlarge: liberate.
enround: surround.
erne: grieve.
even (noun): plain truth (2.1.118).
even (adj.): (i) steady, calm
   (2.2.3); (ii) straightforward
   (4.8.104).
evenly: undeviatingly.
even-pleached: made of
   boughs evenly trimmed and
   inter-woven.
exception: objection.
executors: (i) executioners;
   (ii) legal executors.
exeunt (Latin): they go out.
exhale!: draw out your sword!
exit (Latin): he or she goes out.

face out: intimidate.
fallow: arable land.
farce: stuff, pad out.
fat-brained: dull, stupid.
favour: (i) token worn;
   (ii) appearance.
feared: frightened (1.2.155).
fer: probably 'fear', meaning
   'put fear into', as well as a
   threatening repetition of the
   surname, Fer.

ferret: tear at, like a ferret worrying its prey.

fet: fetched.

fig, figo: obscene gesture in which the thumb is thrust between two of the closed fingers (or in which the thumb is put into the mouth).

firk: beat.

fleshed: initiated into (or inured to) the taste of blood.

flexure: bowing.

flourish (noun): trumpet fanfare.

flower-de-luce: fleur-de-lis.

foils: light swords for fencers.

footed, be: have a foothold.

forage: glut (himself).

force (vb.): cram, pack.

fore-hand: upper hand, advantage.

fox: sword.

fracted: broken.

framed: constructed.

French crown: (a) French gold coin, (b) French head.

French hose: loose wide breeches.

fumitory: weed (plant of the genus *Fumaria*).

gage: pledge, token.

gall: (i) harass, chafe; (ii) scoff (at).

galls: gall-bladders, thought to be the source of bitterness (2.2.30).

Gallia: (i) France; (ii) French.

galliard: lively dance.

gape: desire eagerly.

general (adj.): public (4.1.229).

gentle (vb,): promote to the rank of gentleman.

gesture: posture, deportment.

giddy: fickle, uncertain.

gimmaled: hinged or jointed.

gipes: gibes.

gleeking and galling at: mocking and irritating.

gloze: gloss, interpret.

Go to!: 'Clear off!' (a contemptuous dismissal).

God-a-mercy!: Thank you!

God buy you: Goodbye (God be with you).

God-den: Good evening.

grafter: tree from which a scion has been taken for grafting.

great-belly doublet: doublet with its lower part amply stuffed with bombast.

greenly: as if love-sick.

groat: coin of very low value.

guidon: standard or pennant.

gull (noun): simpleton.

gull (vb.): dupe.

gum: viscous oozing.

gun-stone: cannon-ball.

haggled over: hacked about.

hard-favoured: ugly.

Harflew: Harfleur.

hazard: (a) aperture in the rear wall of a tennis-court (a ball struck into it became unplayable), (b) jeopardy.

hazard, go to: lay a bet.

heady: headstrong.

heir general: legal heir, whether by the male or female line.

hemlock: poisonous weed.

hilding (adj.): sorry, mean.
housewifery: thrift.
humorous: capricious.
humour: (i) mood, inclination;
(ii) character. **Run bad
humours**: display ill-will.
husbandry: (i) housekeeping,
farm management; (ii) crops
(5.2.39).
huswife (pronouced '*huzz*-if '):
hussy, fickle woman.
Hydra-headed: multifarious.
The mythical Hydra was a
beast with nine heads; for
every head cut off, two new
ones grew.

Iceland dog: long-haired lap-
dog.
idly: vainly, foolishly.
imbar: bar.
impawn: pledge.
impeachment: hindrance.
imputation of: accusation of
responsibility for.
indifferently: tolerably.
indirectly: unjustly.
infect: taint.
instance: motive.
intendment: ambition, purpose,
project.
intertissued: interwoven.
investing: including.

jack-an-apes: monkey.
Jack-sauce: impudent fellow.
jade: horse, nag.
jealous: apprehensive.
jealousy: suspicion.
Jewry: Judea.

kecksies: dry hollow stems.
kern: Irish soldier.

lackey: running servant.
larding: enriching.
largess: bounty.
lavolta: lively dance.
law (exclamation and/or
intensifier): so I swear.
lazar: leper.
lea: arable land.
learn you by rote: teach you
by repetition.
legerity: agility.
let (noun): hindrance.
liege: lord.
life: exact likeness (4.2.54).
lig: lie.
like: alike (2.2.183).
linstock: staff to hold a gunner's
lighted match.
lob down: hang down.
lodging: (i) lying down;
(ii) place of lying down.
luxurious: lecherous.
luxury: lust.

manners: moral conduct
(1.2.49).
marches: border regions
(1.2.140).
maw: stomach.
measure: (a) metre, (b) stately
dance, (c) amount (5.2.133-4).
meet (adj.): fitting.
memorable: commemorated,
commemorative.
mervailous: alternative spelling
of 'marvellous' (stressed on
second syllable).
mettle: spirit, courage, character.

mickle: much.

mirror: model, pattern.

miscreate: illegitimate, spurious.

mistful: dim with tears, moist.

mock (vb.): cheat (1.2.286-7).

model to: small-scale replica of.

modest: moderate.

moiety: half.

mope: wander aimlessly.

moral: (i) symbolic figure;
(ii) moral conclusion.

morris-dance: traditional rural dance by groups of costumed dancers.

mortified: killed.

mould, men of: men of clay; mere mortals.

mounted, are: soar (4.1.103-4).

Muse of fire: force of inspiration with fire's ability to soar.

native: (i) proper, rightful;
(ii) in one's own country.

natural: filial.

nature: (i) normal appearance, (ii) the natural feelings of humanity (3.1.8).

neglected: negligently disregarded.

neighbourhood: neighbourly feeling.

nice: scrupulous, punctilious.

nicely: (i) sophistically (1.2.15);
(ii) particularly, punctiliously (5.2.95).

noble (coin): coin of large value.

nook-shotten: (a) misshapen, (b) furtively-engendered.

ordinance: (i) practice, usage;
(ii) ordnance: artillery.

orisons: prayers, pleas.

Orleance: Orléans.

paction: pact, contract.

pale (vb.): enclose, encircle.

palfrey: usually, a smaller saddle-horse; but the palfrey in Act 3, scene 7, is also called a courser.

Paris-balls: tennis-balls.

parle, parley (noun): dialogue with an enemy.

part: (i) (a) the melody assigned to one of the voices or instruments; (b) function, share; (ii) side, party.

pass: indulge in (2.1.122).

pastern: hoof (3.7.12), though normally the part just above the hoof.

pauca (Latin): few (words).

pax: tablet kissed by Catholic communicants.

pennon: ensign, flag or streamer.

perdurable: lasting.

perdy: by God.

peremptory: final.

perpend: weigh.

perspectively: as if it were a perspective, i.e. an artefact which yields one image (or a confused image) when seen from one angle and a different image (or a clear image) when seen from another.

Phoebus: the sun.

pioner: sapper.

pitch and pay: pay cash.

plain-song: simple melody or theme without variations.

plebeian: low born, of the common people.

pocketing-up of wrongs:
(a) receiving stolen goods,
(b) submitting to insults.

policy: (i) statecraft; (ii) intrigue.

popular: of the common people.

popularity: association with the common people.

poring: (a) eye-straining, (b) pouring, pervasive.

port (of Mars): bearing, posture (of the war-god).

portage: port-holes.

possess: inspire, instil (4.1.107, 280).

powdering-tub: (properly) vat for salting beef; (colloquially) sweating-tub used in treating venereal disease.

practic: practical.

practice: plot.

practise on: worked on.

precépt: writ of summons.

preposterously: contrary to the natural order.

prescript: prescribed (3.7.43).

present: immediate.

presently: at once.

pretty and sweet: proper and pleasing (4.6.28).

prey, in: engaged in seeking prey.

profitable: useful.

projection: scale, design.

proportion (noun): (i) levy; (ii) decorum, due measure, harmony.

proportion (vb.): be commensurate with.

pudding: meal of stuffed guts (as in black pudding; 2.1.84).

puissance: armed force, strength.

puissant: powerful, formidable.

purchase (noun): booty (3.2.40).

purgèd judgement: unbiased assessment.

put up: raise (5.2.37).

quality: (i) profession; (ii) efficacy, power.

question (noun): consideration (1.1.5).

quick: alive, living.

quit: (i) absolve; (ii) rid.

quittance: return, recompense.

quotidian tertian: The 'quotidian' was a fever with a paroxysm occurring every day; the tertian was a fever with a paroxysm occurring every other day. The combination of the two was deemed particularly dangerous.

raught: reached out.

rawly left: left abruptly and without provision.

re-answer: repay.

rebuke: check.

reduce: lead back, restore (5.2.63).

reek: ascend like vapour or smoke.

religiously: scrupulously.

relish: taste, flavour, character.

rendezvous: (i) resort, home to return to; (ii) conclusion.

renown (vb.): bring renown to (1.2.118).

repent: regret (2.2.152).
rest (noun): final resolve (2.1.15).
rheum: phlegm.
rim: peritoneum, the serous membrane lining the abdominal cavity and forming a cover for the abdominal organs.
rivage: shore.
Roan: Rouen.
robustious: violent.
roping: hanging like rope.
round: plain-spoken (4.1.195).
rub (noun): obstacle, hindrance (a term from the game of bowls).
run: discharged (2.1.117).

sack: wine (2.3.26).
sad-eyed: serious-looking.
sand: sandbank.
savage: uncultivated, untamed.
savagery: wild growth.
'Sblood: By God's blood.
scaffold: stage.
scambling (vb.): scrambling, struggling, fighting.
scambling (adj.): disorderly, turbulent.
scauld: scabby, scruffy, base.
scion: slip for grafting.
sconce: redoubt, earthwork.
scour: (i) wash away; (ii) (a) scourge, punish severely, (b) clean out, by running a sword through a person as if it were a scouring-rod for cleaning a pistol-barrel.
seat: throne (1.1.36, 88).
secure: carefree, confident (4. Prologue, 17).

security: confidence.
self: self-same (1.1.1).
sennet: trumpet-signal for a formal exit.
sequestration: seclusion.
severals: details, particulars.
shales: shells.
shog: go, move.
show my sail of greatness: display fully my majesty.
shrewdly: sharply, vigorously.
signal: sign of distinction, badge of honour.
silling: shilling (coin or sum).
sinister: left-handed, irregular.
sink: sewer.
sirrah: sir (when addressing an inferior).
skirr: scurry.
slander: scandal, disgrace.
slips, in the: on the leash.
slobbery: sloppy, wet.
slough: old skin (which can be cast off, like that of snakes).
sodden: boiled.
solus (Latin): alone.
sonance: (probably) resonant.
sort: (i) rank, degree; (ii) style, array.
spin: spurt.
spital: charitable hospital, especially one for low-class people and those afflicted with foul diseases; lazar-house.
spoil: ruin (4.5.18).
square of battle: square military formation.
stand off: stand out.
sternage: the sterns.
still (adv.): constantly.

stomach: taste, inclination, appetite.

stoop: swoop down (like a hawk) upon some object.

strike (vb.): fight (2.4.54).

strossers: trousers; **strait strossers**: tight trousers.

suddenly: quickly.

sufferance: (i) suffering (2.2.159); (ii) patience (3.6.121); **by his sufferance**: by the mercy shown him (2.2.46).

suit (vb.): clothe (4.2.53).

sumless: incalculable.

summer (vb.): nurture.

sur-reined: over-ridden, over-worked.

sutler: one who sells provisions to the army.

swasher: swaggerer.

sworn brothers: soldiers who take an oath to share each other's good and bad fortunes.

sympathise with: resemble (3.7.133).

take: (a) take fire, (b) strike (2.1.50).

take up short: give short shrift to, give a decisive response to.

tall: valiant (2.1.66).

'tame (attame): rend.

Tartar: Tartarus, the classical hell.

task (vb.): earnestly preoccupy.

tell (at 5.2.191): (a) judge, (b) say.

temper (vb.): mould (2.2.118).

tender (vb,): hold dear (2.2.175).

tenour: substance, purport.

terms: **in fair terms, in good terms**: (a) in plain language, (b) quite thoroughly. **Stand on terms**: insist on conditions.

testament: will.

theoric: theory.

train: retinue.

Troyan: foreign warrior (or, less likely, 'dissolute roisterer').

troth-plight: engaged, formally pledged to marry.

trumpet: trumpeter (4.7.49).

truth: **firm truth of valour**: steadfastly honourable courage.

tucket: trumpet-call.

tun: barrel.

turn head: turn to face an enemy.

tyke: cur.

umbered: shadowed, darkened.

uncoined: unminted, not in common use.

unfurnished: unequipped, unprepared.

unprovided: unprepared.

unraisèd: uninspired.

untempering: uningratiating, unsoftening.

use: treat (3.2.120–21).

vary: express in a variety of ways.

vasty: vast, wide.

vaultage: cavern.

vaward: vanguard.

venture trade: speculate in trade.

verify in his beard: tell him to his face.

verily: truly.
vile: mean, of low rank.
voice: acclamation, vote
  (2.2.113).
void: quit (4.7.52).
vulgar (noun): common people.

wafer-cakes: very thin pastry,
  like the wafers used in the
  Mass.
war-proof, of: proven in war.
wasteful: devastating.
wax (vb.): grow.
wear: possess and enjoy (5.2.228).
whelks: pimples.
whiffler: officer who clears the
  way for a procession.
white-livered: 'lily-livered',
  cowardly.
wide: capacious and welcoming
  to corruption (3.3.13).

wink: (i) close both eyes;
  (ii) close one eye in a wink
  (5.2.299).
word: motto (2.3.45).
working-house: workshop.
worshipped: honoured (1.2.234).
wrack: wreckage.
wrangler: adversary, disputant.
wringing: pain.

yeoman: 'a commoner or
  countryman of respectable
  standing, esp. one who
  cultivates his own land'
  (O.E.D.).
yerk: kick.
yoke-fellow: equally-matched
  companion.